SEPARATION *from the* WORLD

SEPARATION
from the
WORLD

SHOULD A CHRISTIAN VOTE?

Joseph John Bowman

Copyright © 2019 by Joseph John Bowman.

PAPERBACK: 978-1-7340699-2-1
EBOOK: 978-1-7340699-3-8

All rights reserved. No part of this publication may be reproduced, distributed, or transmitted in any form or by any electronic or mechanical means, without the prior written permission of the publisher, except in the case of brief quotations embodied in critical reviews and certain other noncommercial uses permitted by copyright law.

All Scripture quotations – unless otherwise stated – are from the King James Version of the Bible. (It is known as the Authorized Version.)

Ordering Information:

For orders and inquiries, please contact:
1-888-375-9818
www.toplinkpublishing.com
bookorder@toplinkpublishing.com

Printed in the United States of America

The following papers are by the same author:

1. Heaven, My Celestial Home
2. The Gospel According to John 3:16
3. Biblical Divorce & Remarriage
4. Separation from the Word – Should a Christian Vote?
5. The World, The Believers Outward Foe

CONTENTS

Prologue ix
Annotation xiii
Acknowledgments... xix
Preface... xxiii
Introduction.. xxix

Chapter One – Political Separation in the Past 1

Chapter Two – Separation of the Nazarites.........................9
   1. Separation of the Nazarite – Unto the Lord 13
      i)   Separation unto our Salvation 14
      ii)   Separating to Worship Him..................................15
      iii) Separating to His Authority 15
      iv) Separation in our Service 16
      v)   Matrimonial Separation..18
      vi) Separation in our Private Lives 19
      vii) Separation in our Prayers 20
      viii) Separation in our Sorrows...................................22
   2. Separation of the Nazarite – Worldly Joys 26
   3. Separation of the Nazarite – Earthly Shame 30
   4. Separation of the Nazarite – Purity........................38

Chapter Three – Separation of Abraham 45
   1. Political Separation 48
   2. Social Separation..57
   3. Religious Separation 61

Chapter Four – Separation in 2 Cor. 6 65
   1. Separation of the Believer in 2 Corinthians 6 66

Chapter Five – The Five Subjects in 2 Corinthians 6:14-16 69
   1. A Commercial Union Condemned......................................69
   2. A Social Union Condemned 75
   3. A Political Union Condemned 84
   4. An Ecclesiastical Union Condemned 85
   5. A Matrimonial Union Condemned 89

Chapter Six – Political Separation 94
   Christ – The Sent One 98
   Christ – Our Leader...103
   Belial – Satan's Leader 111
   The Wickedness of Government... 121
   Is God in Control? 126
   The Believer's Responsibility on Earth 137
   Our Responsibility – To the Union.....................................149
   The Servant Master Relationship.......................................156
   The Responsibility of Christian Employers.......................... 161

Conclusion... 165
Finis... 169
Culmination 177
Bibliography... 181
Biography 183

PROLOGUE

The subject of this book is dealing with separation. It is a big subject dealing with every aspect of a believers life. If we do not give ourselves entirely to God, we will not be able to be used by Him.

We sometimes say,

> "If He is not Lord of all, He is not Lord at all."

The above is full of Truth. "How can we call Him our Lord and rebel against His rule?"

We are asked:

> "Why call ye Me, Lord, Lord, and do not the things which I say?" (Luke 6:46).

It is a question that has to have an answer. We cannot acknowledge Him as Lord and then disregard His commands. One who is Lord is in total and absolute control. He is the pre-eminent ruler. We cannot challenge His commands. It should be self-evident what our response should be. The only question should be, "How should I accomplish His will in my life?" Otherwise, we are acting in rebellion to the will of God. That will is brought out in our separation from this world and all its sins and rebellion.

Initially, we must separate ourselves unto God. Only then will God be able to use us in His work. We will be useful servants in His kingdom. To be engaged in His service in this world takes one other step. We must be separate from this world. Everything in it is at enmity with

Joseph John Bowman

God. All that is in it is of the Wicked One. He aims to destroy the works of God on this earth. The means of accomplishing that goal is to destroy the testimonies of the people of God. Our defense is to live in fellowship with the One who has redeemed our souls. We are bought with the precious blood of He, who is the Lamb of God. He desires that we live in service to Him every day. For that to happen, we must live lives separate from all the attractions of this world. We may not think we are indulging in the depths of its sins; however, if we are engaged in its follies and pleasures, we are enjoying the fruits of this world. We often say that we cannot walk the line. Either we are serving Him who is our Saviour or we are living under the control of the Prince of the Power of the Air. There is no other way we can go.

I can remember my mother-in-law, saying that "Success among the people of God comes down to one word (or maybe two). It is submission or obedience to the will of God. If we submit to Him and His will for us, we will experience His blessings.

I want to give a hymn about the blessings we can experience from God. It is "Count Your Blessings."

Gypsy Smith, a famous evangelist of the times, said of this song, "Men sing it, boys whistle it and women rock their babies to sleep to it."

This hymn was a source of help and encouragement to the Lord's people over the years. Singing the truths given in the song is one thing. Realizing them in our lives is another. The only way to experience the blessings of God in our lives is to submit to Him and His will for us. We will be living our lives in obedience to Him and separate from the world that hates Him. Otherwise, our lives will be false representations what we claim to believe.

I trust it will be to us here as well,

Separation from the World

Count Your Blessings

"When upon life's billows you are tempest-tossed,
When you are discouraged, thinking all is lost,
Count your many blessings, name them one by one,
And it will surprise you what the Lord has done.

Refrain

Count your blessings, name them one by one,
Count your blessings, see what God has done!
Count your blessings, name them one by one,
And it will surprise you what the Lord has done.

Are you ever burdened with a load of care?
Does the cross seem heavy you are called to bear?
Count your many blessings, every doubt will fly,
And you will keep singing as the days go by.

When you look at others with their lands and gold,
Think that Christ has promised you His wealth untold,
Count you many blessings – money cannot buy,
Your reward in Heaven, nor your Home on high.

So amid the conflict whether great or small,
Do not be discouraged, God is over all;
Count your many blessings, angels will attend,
Help and comfort give you to your journeys end.

Johnson Oatman Jr.

ANNOTATION

The subject is one that has been often discussed many times over the years. Sadly, it is seldom even considered today. It is considered to be an unsolvable subject. The brethren look at anyone who brings it up as being a cause of division and dissension. I hope to look at this subject in a manner that is both scriptural as well as profitable for every believer. The aim of this work is that the Saints are strengthened and the local gatherings of believers testimonies encouraged and found to the glory of God.

We will be looking at Christians becoming involved in government. The question will be whether it is appropriate for a Christian to vote? The stand of most Christians is that it is not only appropriate for Christians to vote; it is our responsibility.

Therefore, those who do not vote have failed in their responsibility to act as an agent of change in this world. That failure is seen both before God, as well as before, man. By taking this stand, we are placing responsibility on believers dealing with both the present governance of these countries as well as decisions made that will affect the future. We are told decisions, and the repercussions that follow are ours to make. If we do not enter into these discussions and take the applicable stands, we will be failing in our duty before God in this world. If we do not publicly defend the doctrines of Scripture, we will be failing our duty on earth before God. Although, not being said in so many words, the implication is that God is unable to work His will without our input into the political decisions of the day. If there are failure and departure from the Word of God and His will for us, it is because of the departure of the people of God.

Joseph John Bowman

By saying these things, we are placing a tremendous responsibility on the Lord's people. More importantly, we are stating that God is unable to fulfill His work of grace and judgment on this earth without our participation. In the end, we deny the truths of Scripture. The world is on a downward slope. In the end, it will be judged and destroyed by God for its godless actions and decisions. The hearts of humanity are against God. Because of their enmity to God, humanity will be judged.

The reason God has left His people on this earth is not to slow down humanities demoralization or to make them better. It is to present to them the love of God through the work of the Lord Jesus on the cross. They are told that if they reject this message, they will face eternal judgment. No amount of social engineering or betterment of society will change that condemnation by God. It will not matter one bit whether or not the pollution on the earth is less than it is now. It does not matter whether man's moral decisions or actions are changed if their heart remains in enmity to God. Since all of humanity is under the curse of sin, we are all under the judgment of God.

We have these words of condemnation given by Paul to the Romans.

> "All have sinned, and come short of the glory of God"
> (Rom. 3:23).

Not only are we condemned as sinners, but we are told why we are in this state as well as the end facing each one of us.

> "Wherefore, as by one man sin entered into the world,
> and death by sin; and so death has passed upon all
> men, for that all have sinned" (Rom. 5:12).

Despite our deplorable condition, Almighty God has provided a way of escape. It is only through the work of Him who came into this world to be our Saviour.

Separation from the World

Because of His work, He can say,

> "They that are whole have no need of the physician,
> but they that are sick: I came not to call the righteous,
> but sinners to repentance" (Mark 2:17).

Moreover, He said,

> "For the Son of Man is come to seek and to save that
> which is lost" (Luke 19:10).

We are not here to be the social or moral conscience of this world. We are not to make or urge the unsaved to live better lives. We are their condemnation when they see their evil works. The Lord Jesus told His disciples that this was to be one of the works of the Holy Spirit when He came into this world,

> "And when He is come, He will reprove the world of sin,
> and of righteousness, and of judgment: of sin, because
> they believe not on Me: of righteousness, because I go to
> My Father, and ye see Me no more: of judgment, because
> the Prince of this World is judged" (John 16:8-11).

Since this is the work the Spirit of God is doing on this earth, why should we feel that our work is any different? What makes us think that by changing the actions and decisions of this world morally and socially, they can be changed?

Nothing is accomplished if a soul goes to Hell despite their charitable works. Many Churches are seeking to make humanity better. They are involved in all manner of charities and social programs. The feeling of many, if not most, is that it would be unjust for God to condemn them. They feel that their good works will outweigh their bad. The thought is that in that final day, there will be a calculation. When all of their good works are accumulated, they will get into Heaven, or be consigned to Hell. It is salvation wrought by good works. In their thoughts, they have no dependence on the work of Christ on the cross.

Joseph John Bowman

Many Christians tacitly reinforce their false conceptions. They are seen encouraging various activities as they seek to work towards the betterment of humanity. While there is nothing wrong in seeking the betterment of humanity, that is not the believer's mission. Many poor souls are working their way to Heaven, not knowing they are fast on the road to Hell. Unfortunately, they are being deceived by the very believers who should be teaching them the error of their ways.

> "Not by works of righteousness which we have done, but according to His mercy, He saved us" (Titus 3:5).

Years before Isaiah said;

> "But we are all as an unclean thing, and all our righteousnesses are as filthy rags: and we all do fade as a leaf: and our iniquities, like the wind, have taken us away" (Is. 64:6).

A sister I know told the account of her grandmother. She had been told that she was a sinner condemned to Hell. However, she was secure in her righteous acts. One day she was on her knees washing the floor. As she looked at the rags being used to do the work, the Spirit of God brought before her the truth that the best she could do was no better than the filthy rags in her wash bucket. At that moment, she accepted the work done for her on the cross. She acknowledged that she was the sinner for whom Christ died. She took the position of the godless individual in Luke.

The Lord Jesus told of two men who went into the Temple to pray to God. The first was confident in his extraordinary life and actions. However, there was a second man. He recognized that he was a sinner and needed the forgiveness of a righteous God.

> "And the publican, (sinner whose life was identified by sinful acts – Ed.). standing afar off, would not lift up so much as his eyes unto Heaven, but smote upon his breast, saying, God be merciful to me a sinner. I

Separation from the World

tell you, this man went down to his house justified rather than the other" (Luke 18:13-14).

The unsaved need to be told of their lost condition. Only then can these lost souls come to the One who can save even those who are among the most wicked in society. Upon that action, a change will take place in their hearts and lives that will be of a positive effect to all humanity. Only then will the world see evidence of the power and love of God in this world.

The responsibility of every believer is to teach those among us to be separate from the sins of this world. It is not to seek to correct the sins of humanity.

> "As obedient children, not fashioning yourselves according to the former lusts in your ignorance: but as He which hath called you is holy, so be ye holy in all manner of conversation (lifestyle – Ed.): because it is written, be ye holy, for I am holy. And if ye call on the Father, Who without respect of persons judgeth according to every mans work, pass the time of your sojourning (life – Ed.) here in fear: forasmuch as ye know that ye were not redeemed with corruptible things, such as silver and gold, from your vain conversation (empty manner of life – Ed.) received by tradition from your fathers: but with the precious blood of Christ, as of a Lamb without blemish and without spot" (1 Pet. 1:14-19).

We need to acknowledge that the instruction to holy living is to all believers. It has nothing to do with the world. Their manner of life is wicked and against God. There is nothing that pleases God among them. Therefore, we can do nothing to make them more pleasing to God. The only thing that can be done is to experience the New Birth. They must be saved! That is our responsibility among them. It is not for us to seek social and moral improvement in their midst. Entering into the governments and parliaments of this world will not affect the outcome God has determined for this world one little bit.

ACKNOWLEDGMENTS

I want to start by expressing a deep sense of gratitude to my dear wife, Joanie. She has allowed me to have the time necessary to prepare this work. I have spent much time studying and looking into the various aspects of this subject as I prepared it for the public. I am so thankful for the spiritual help and support she provided.

As well, I want to express my appreciation to Joanie for her help in editing this work. She has read it numerous times. She has corrected grammatical and spelling errors. She has also, in many instances, made the text more understandable. Places that were not clear have been changed so that they may be more readily understood. In the end, it is unprofitable to seek to teach if the subject is not apparent to those to whom it is directed. It is not always easy and takes time. I owe her a deep debt of gratitude for all she has done.

Before I acknowledge the help given by other believers, I desire to thank God for all He has shown. Indeed, the Spirit of God is our Teacher; He is the One who teaches all truth. We would be unable to learn any of the truths of the things of God without His intercession on our behalf. It is because of Him we can seek the deep things of God.

We are exhorted to learn the truths of Scripture by the apostle Paul where he said,

> "Study to show thyself approved unto God, a workman that needeth not to be ashamed, rightly dividing the Word of Truth" (2 Tim. 2:15).

Joseph John Bowman

Although I was involved in this work, I want to acknowledge the ministry of a brother recently. He is Alan Smith of Scotland. He was ministering on this subject. I found what he had to say very informative. While he backed up my views on these points, I appreciated his viewpoint. It gave me a feeling a justification as well as having a Scriptural basis for the points in this book.

There have been many others whose ministry in both the public as well as the private forums has been influential in the book. Although I am unable to name them all, I want to acknowledge that no knowledge is attained without help from other believers. That is because part of the work of believers in a public gathering is to feed one another. We are to seek to see each other grow in the things of the Lord.

There is a saying in the world,

> "No man is an island."

Nowhere is it more accurate than in spiritual things.

Unfortunately, some brethren seem to think they do not need the ministry of other brethren to guide them into the truths of God. They think that they will be able to learn all they need on their own. Paul sought to dismiss this teaching with the following words,

> "And the things that thou hast heard of me among many
> witnesses, the same commit thou to faithful men, who
> shall be able to teach others also" (2 Tim. 2:2)

One of our highly respected workers, John Abernathy, once said,

> "You can always tell the self-taught man; he is the one
> who does not know anything."

Even the world will beware of any contact with the man who cannot be taught by others. That is because they are dangerous. For a little

Separation from the World

knowledge is a dangerous thing in the hands of a man who does not know how to use it with wisdom.

The above is a quotation from as early as the 1600s. I want to give a few of the variations in this place. Reading them, let us apply these thoughts to the reception and application of Scripture in the local Church and the daily lives of every individual believer.

A proverb goes,

> "A little knowledge is a dangerous thing expresses the idea that a small amount of knowledge can mislead people into thinking that they are more expert than they really are, which can lead to mistakes being made."

The content of the above has been attributed to Alexander Pope.

However, even before him an anonymous author signing himself A.B. published the following in 1698 in his "The Mystery of Phanaticism.

> "Twas well observed by my Lord Bacon, that a little knowledge is apt to puff up, and make me giddy, but a greater share of it will set them right, and bring them to low and humble thoughts of themselves."

The Lord Bacon referred to was the English politician and philosopher Viscount St. Alban. He was a man of learning who is recognized even to this day. Bacon wrote the following,

> "A little philosophy inclineth man's mind to atheism: but depth in philosophy bringeth men's minds about to religion."

Lastly, there is a quotation by Alexander Pope.

> "A little learning is a dangerous thing; drink deep, or taste not the Pierian spring: their shallow draughts

Joseph John Bowman

> intoxicate the brain, and drinking largely sobers us
> again."

(The Pierian spring in Greek mythology, was the source of knowledge, art, and science. By drinking of it, the person who partook of its cooling waters received of the knowledge and wisdom that was given forth from its depths.)

The teaching is the same in every one of these quotations. Before becoming a teacher of the knowledge received, make sure that we have fully understood and appreciated its benefits. Otherwise, we may cause more harm than good to those around us.

Paul gives a warning concerning those who seek to teach. There were numbered among them those whose understanding of the Scriptures is lacking or misguided.

I trust that we will not fall into the category of those Paul is telling Timothy.

> "From which some having swerved have turned aside
> unto vain jangling; desiring to be teachers of the law;
> understanding neither what they say, nor whereof they
> affirm. But we know that the law is good, if a man use
> it lawfully" (1 Tim. 1:6-8).

At the end of this section, I will leave the warning that James gave to each of us who take the place of leadership and as teachers among the people of God. We have assumed a work that is far-reaching and has enormous consequences both now and in the future. Keep in mind the influence given among those whom we mix. Take this with all seriousness and consider the words of James.

> "My brethren, be not many masters, knowing that we
> shall receive the greater condemnation" (James 3:1).

PREFACE

Today, probably more than in any other time in history, believers are obsessed with their opportunities to influence governments. In past years, most governments were different types of Monarchies or Dictatorships. They were ruled with a hand of iron. No dissension was allowed. Anyone with a view that differed from the ruling party was punished severely. Any marches or displays of public disobedience was promptly put down. Military intervention was not uncommon. People naturally, and the saints, in general, were unable to make their views known on any subjects. The governments and religions of the day forced everyone to agree with the beliefs commonly held. Demonstrators were imprisoned and even put to death. They were charged with treason for daring to differ from the government of the day. The same charges and conditions applied to those who voiced their dissatisfaction with the church of the day. Ordinary people were kept in a place of subservience. There was no freedom of expression or speech. The freedom and independence of the press were absent. Freedom of religion was unknown. Only the recognized national church was allowed. The citizenry of the various countries had no freedom. They were treated abominably.

Despite these conditions, the Church of God grew and strengthened. Souls were saved and went on for God. It was especially evident after the invention of the printing press. From then on the ordinary people had the Bible in their language. They were able to read and understand the Word of God for themselves. Through it, all the believers experienced terrible persecution. God promised He would bless them, and they would receive the martyrs crown.

Joseph John Bowman

In most western countries this persecution has come to an end. However, there are indications that persecution against believers could re-emerge. I want to give some statistics dealing with the persecution of Christians worldwide in 2018.

Reading of the troubles these Saints are going through, keep in mind the words of the apostle Paul.

> "And if one member suffers, all the members suffer with it; or if one member be honored, all the members rejoice with it" (1 Cor. 12:26).

The following came off of the Open Doors USA website. It is an organization established to help believers suffering under the scourge of persecution.

These are some of the statistics for believers in 2018.

> "Christians remain one of the most persecuted religious groups in the world. Christian torture remains an issue for believers throughout the world, including the risk of imprisonment, loss of home and assets, physical torture, beheadings, rape, and even death as a result of their faith. Worldwide, 1 in 9 Christians experiences high levels of persecution. North Korea is ranked #1 for the 18th year in a row as the most dangerous country for Christians. Christians are one of the most persecuted religious groups in the world and are oppressed in at least 60 countries.

Every month on average:

a) 345 Christians are killed for faith-related reasons.
b) 105 Churches and Christians buildings are burned or attacked.
c) 219 Christians are detained without trial, arrested, sentenced, and imprisoned."

Separation from the World

Considering the persecution undergone by many of the Lord's people, we need to ask, "What makes us so special?"

With that in mind, I want to give the headline and a few lines from an article by a Southern Baptist leader about the work of the Lord in China. The headline of his article read,

"CHINESE CHRISTIANS ARE PRAYING THAT PERSECUTION COMES TO THE AMERICAN CHURCH"

"So it can experience the revival that is sweeping China."

The article revealed that the Chinese house Church movement is praying that American Christians might experience the kind of persecution they have seen in China so that it would ignite a similar revival in America. Draper, the Baptist leader, said that a reporter asked a local leader how American Churches could pray for the house Churches in China. Here was the response.

"Stop praying for persecution in China to end, for it is through persecution that the Church has grown." The man then continued by saying, "In fact, we are praying that the American Church might taste the same persecution, so revival would come to the American Church like we have seen in China."

Democracies now rule many countries. Their governments are elected and kept in power by the will of the people. Many Christians feel they should participate in the election of their ruler's and engage in government in this way. Some even enter into the political forum and run as candidates. It is an area that is highly controversial. Christians come under immense pressure to support the candidate who supports their beliefs. They justify their stands by saying we

Joseph John Bowman

have a responsibility in this way. That opportunity was not offered to the early believers. It is held unquestioningly that we should take advantage of this privilege. We have this opportunity to voice our opinions, either for or against any political stands. The stand is that we have been given an opportunity we should take to our advantage.

Many believers take part in marches and demonstrations against the government of the day. They take forceful, and sometimes illegal, stands against various laws. They seek to influence the making of laws by wielding financial power. They threaten to withhold their votes from a candidate who does not fall in line. In all of this, Christians are pitted against other Christians. Because of things said, and stands taken testimonies are lost. Furthermore, the name of Christ is brought into disrepute.

There was recently a provincial election in the province of Alberta where I live. During the campaign, several candidates had to withdraw because they publicly stated they held beliefs that were grounded in Scripture. Such a public outcry was raised that they were forced to withdraw their names from consideration. The same can be said about believers who are holding public office in any country around the world. If they stand up for what is right, they will be ostracized, and never be reelected again.

In some cases, the name of Christ is spoken of with disrespect in the world. Sadly, most of these believers are woefully unaware of how they appear in the eyes of the world. They have one aim in view. Hopefully, they will be able to sway the government to make rules aligned with the teaching of the Bible. They can then influence our society for good. By so doing, they will be testimonies for God and seek to slow down the pervasive influences of evil coming among us. They can then have power over the making and outworking of laws. By so doing the forces of evil will be destroyed. We are putting ourselves in a position of power that was unknown to early believers.

Practically speaking the only time the Church experienced this power and influence was from the days of Constantine to the Reformation.

Separation from the World

Power and wealth, along with unlimited influence, were given to them. However, the Church abused their position. They became as bad as those who had persecuted them in the years before. In some ways, they were even worse. It was because they were holding the position and work of spiritual guides to the people. By abusing their position, they became a source of hatred and contempt.

There is a saying in the world. It applies wherever people hold power, especially unlimited power. It is as applicable to believers and the Church of God as anyone else.

> "Power corrupts, and absolute power corrupts absolutely."

INTRODUCTION

At the start of this paper, I want to deal with an important topic. It deals with an area of separation from the world often ignored by many Christians. They believe we are to live separated lives. However, when it comes to the political arena, they make a difference. In this area, as in all others, God wants separation. We are not to be united, or go into any form of partnership with it.

Many Christians feel strongly about voting. While they may not want to run for political office, they see nothing wrong with trying to elect politicians. In some parts of the country, the Christian right is such a force politically that politicians will do or say anything to get their votes. Christians in these areas often place their votes as a block for the politician whose stands on things like abortion and the death penalty coincides with theirs. Some of the public statements they make about some of the sins of humanity only cause those in the world to hate them. Unfortunately, they earn their names of racists, gay-bashers, and homophobes, among others. They feel justified by their actions. Their judgmental attitudes are evident to the world around them.

The question needs asking,

> "Can we tell the world that God loves them and wants to save them when we are showing by our public actions how much we despise them and their lifestyles?"

That in no way excuses the sins of humanity. It is not a change in lifestyle that is needed. It is a change of heart. Only then will the

Joseph John Bowman

manner of their lives change. Many Christians are seeking to change the way governments run. When their man or woman is elected, they will try to influence the policies of the country in the way that they believe is best for them. Some believers bring undue influence on the party they have sought to see elected. These pressures are brought to bear in ways such as monetary threats. They threaten that unless the changes they demand are made, the politicians in question will face negative consequences.

There is a significant difference between this attitude and that which Paul exhorted Timothy to show in his letter to him.

> "I exhort therefore, that, first of all, supplications, prayers, intercessions, and giving of thanks, be made for all men; for kings, and for all that are in authority; that we may lead a quiet and peaceable life in all godliness and honesty" (1 Tim. 2:1-2).

It is a fact beyond dispute that if we are praying for the good and benefit of an individual, it will be complicated to move in opposition to them. The desire of God for us is that remembrances be made of them in our prayers. It is not that we raise our hands or fists in opposition to them or to their positions on whatever they may hold.

Unfortunately, many believers seek to influence the choices of those who are the administrative personnel in the country. They seek to put pressure on judges and legal forces in the country to enact the changes they desire. They may engage in marches and sit-ins and other forms of civil disobedience. The methods used are as unsavory and nasty as those used by the groups opposing them. In the end, it is almost impossible to tell the difference between the methods used by either group. Nothing in the way these believer's act is either God-honoring or is the way the Lord acted. He came to save sinners and those despised by society. While He condemned their sins, He did not seek to drive them away. His call was for them to come.

Separation from the World

The other way many believers have of entering into the political forum is by getting involved in the actions of their union. Many believers do not realize the irony of their position. For, while they may abstain from voting politically, they are involved in many aspects of their unions.

I want to look at these different areas and see what the Bible has to say about being involved in them. For when it comes down to brass tacks, as the saying goes, it does not matter the least bit what I might say or think, but it is what God has said in His Word. The only way to do this is to start by looking at some of the Scriptures dealing with this sensitive subject.

CHAPTER ONE – POLITICAL SEPARATION IN THE PAST

The question is, "Whether or not it is right for a believer to be involved in the political forums of this world?"

There is only one way to resolve this subject. We need to see what the Word of God has to say. Looking at this subject, keep in mind that there is hardly a medium that Satan, the Prince of the Power of the World, has more power over than the political setting. Thinking about the wickedness in it, consider, whether, as children of the King, we should be there or not?

From the beginnings of humanity, the first attempts at forming a civilization were in rebellion to God. In Genesis 10:10, there was the formation of Babel along with the cities of Erech, and Accad, and Calneh, all of which were in the land of Shinar. Nimrod founded these cities.

He was

> "A mighty hunter before the Lord" (Gen. 10:9).

The thought seems to be that he was a mighty hunter from before the Lord. In all his activities, he departed from the presence of God. His departure from God is in his building these cities. They were built to make a name for himself. There was no recognition of God in these cities. Their governments did not acknowledge the rule of God. Everything about them was in rebellion to God. Because of that, God judged them.

Joseph John Bowman

A godly brother, Sidney Maxwell, once said that

> "A place started on the wrong grounds will never go right."

How true that was in these cities brought before us!

From, Gen. 11:2-4, the land of Shinar was where they built the tower of Babel. That action indicated their ability and willingness to work in co-operation together. It indicates the beginnings of a political union. God judged it in the following verses. He did it by changing their languages so they could not understand each other. As a result of this one act, they were dispersed over the face of the whole earth. All the different languages upon this earth are because of the judging hand of God.

(Google tells us that there are roughly 6,500 spoken languages in the world today. One study placed the number at 7,111. On top of them, there are tens of thousands of dialects within the spoken language forms.)

Humanity is trying to develop a one-world language that will be understandable to all. Despite all their efforts, they will never entirely succeed. Humanity will never escape the sentence God has imposed upon them because of their sin and rebellion. God has made His opinion of humanity's unions very clear. By seeking, in a misguided way, to try to aid humanity in their illicit desires, we will be working against God. Even if the individual or system we are supporting is Christian in its aims or desires, it is the system that is corrupt, not necessarily every individual involved in it. By entering into the political arena, what transpires will be the working of those involved contrary to the express will of God.

One of the chief means of governing is by compromise. A wise individual will only fight the battles they feel a possibility of winning. A politician's way of winning and gaining political capital for the future is by giving way on those items considered to be of lesser

Separation from the World

importance. In this area, they make concessions for what is felt to be the better good. It is called compromise. Compromise is the standard by which politicians can succeed, and achieve their various goals. It is often at the expense of those who had placed trust in them. In our making agreements, we are dealing with corrupt politicians who are not guided by ethics or morals. What they want is to win. The final result is not one that honors or glorifies God. We barter away aspects of the holiness of God for political advantage. God judged the first civil governmental association in history.

In this line, there is what has been referred to in myth and literature as the ability of a person to sell their souls to the Devil. The main context is that by yielding themselves to the Devil and his power, the person will receive powers and abilities beyond what they previously had. It is the enactment of an unholy union.

The Lord Jesus spoke of the formation of this type of union in the following words.

> "No man can serve two masters; for either he will hate the one, or love the other; or else he will hold to the one, and despise the other, ye cannot serve God and mammon" (or the forces of the the Devil – Ed.). (Matt. 6:24).

Take this warning seriously, since the Lord thought it was worthy of His mention, we need to make sure that it does not become an area we enter.

There was recently an election in the province of Canada where I reside. Sadly, several individuals who were running for their parties were disqualified because of their stands on social programs. In the moral stands of society, they were unacceptable to hold power in the province. It was to be either the one or the other. Either they would renounce their stands by the Word of God, or they would remove themselves from contention in the political arena. The above

3

Joseph John Bowman

is worldwide, and believers need to hold fast to their profession of faith and not compromise for the sake of political expediency.

Every political union has come under God's legislative judgment. Other cities came into being at this time. (See Genesis 10:11-12.) The only one I want to look at besides Babel is Nineveh. It was raised against God and has been in opposition to God ever since its inception. It raised its hand against God continuously, except for one very brief period under Jonah, (Jonah 3:6-9, 4:11) until God destroyed it (Zephaniah 2:13). Throughout history, it was the capital city of the kings of Assyria who were perennial enemies of the people of God. God showed His hatred for all these cities represented. He not only judged Babel in Genesis 11 but ultimately placed the responsibility for all rebellion against this city. The final judgment of Babel or Babylon is in Revelation 17 & 18.

Not only were all these cities aligned against God, but the governments in them were against Him. An example of the government of these cities is in Sodom and Gomorrah. Lot was in the gate of Sodom. The gate of the city always speaks of the administration of the city. In the world, it is always contrary to all that is of God. For their rebellion against Him, God destroyed these cities, and all that pertained to them. God was in opposition to the legislation of those cities In like manner; He is opposed to the principles of every government upon earth. That is because they are all affiliated with the Devil, who is allied with them against God. So, if this is the case, who are we to be in association with the Devil? He was arrayed against the powers of God in the past, and is he any better now? Alternatively, have things gotten any better now than they were in days of old? That being the case, has the current situation shown that things will get better?

The words of Paul are indicative of every age in history. It matters not whether it was when Babel was formed or in this current age of the history of humanity.

> "Evil men and seducers shall wax worse and worse,
> deceiving and being deceived" (2 Tim. 3:13).

Separation from the World

Every believer should be aware that the wickedness of this world will never get any better but worse. Some people elected may be outstanding God-fearing people and desire to do what is right. The times are in God's hands. He has predetermined the end. While we do not know when the end will finally come, it is closer than ever before. Every year brings the end and judgment of this world closer than it was last year. That fact is indisputable. The world was wicked before, and because of their evil actions, God judged it. From Scripture, this is the end that awaits the world today.

God promised in Genesis 8:21-22 He would not destroy the world with a flood as He did in Noah's time. As a guarantee, He gave us a rainbow in the sky. God spoke of this in Genesis 9:11-17. The rainbow reminds us of the grace of God. He promised He would never again curse the world with a worldwide flood. However, it is also a reminder that a holy God judged this world in righteousness. His judgment will come upon this world in a coming day. God will not allow humanity to continue in their wicked ways forever. That day is not coming in a vague, uncertain sense.

God has set it in His calendar.

> "Because He hath appointed a day, in the which He will judge the world in righteousness by that Man Whom He hath ordained: whereof He hath given assurance unto all men, in that He hath raised Him from the dead" (Acts 17:31).

The destruction will not be by the water in a coming day but fire.

> "But the day of the Lord will come as a thief in the night; in the which, the heavens shall pass away with a great noise, and elements shall melt with fervent heat, the earth also and the works that are therein shall be burned up" (2 Pet. 3:10).

Joseph John Bowman

It will be a terrible day. Humanity will be powerless to do anything about it.

Believers are not here to cure the ills of society. Humanity needs to look back in the history of this world and see how things were in the past.

There is a quotation that goes this way.

> "Those who cannot remember the past are doomed to repeat it." (George Santayana – 1905).

It was changed to say,

> "Those who fail to learn from history are condemned to repeat it" (Winston Churchhill, – 1948).

Sadly humanity has neither learned nor sought to repent from the sins of their past. As a result, they are under the indictment of God for their sins. Nothing that anyone can do will cause that action from transpiring. The only thing that will do any good for society, as well as the individuals who make up part of it, is the salvation of those involved.

We will witness how a holy God looks upon sin and the activities and desires of this world and seek to stay as far away from it. Obey the commandments of the Lord and be separate from this world in every area (2 Corinthians. 6:17-18).

Our separation from this world is not an indication that we are vanquished. Defeat is not involved in any part of a Christians life. Victory is in serving our Lord as well as the reason behind His work. Because He is victorious, every believer can take part in His victorious life. Every Saint is a child of the King. Therefore, each one acknowledges that He is King of kings and Lord of lords (Rev. 19:16).

Separation from the World

The hymn writer well put it as he viewed Him whom we serve. He is the One to whom we are separated. It is unto Him we look. Let our praise be to Him who is in Heaven.

Because He is victorious, every believer can take part in His victorious life.

Oh, Worship the King

Oh, worship the King
All glorious above:
Oh, gratefully sing
His power and His love,
Our Shield and Defender,
The Ancient of Days,
Pavilioned in splendor
And girded with praise!

Oh, tell of His might,
Oh, tell of his grace,
Whose robe is the Light,
Whose canopy space!
His chariots of wrath
The deep thunder-clouds form,
And dark is his path
On the wings of the storm.

Thy bountiful care
What tongue can recite?
It breathes in the air,
It shines in the light,
It steams from the hills,
And descends to the plain,
And sweetly distills
In the dew and the rain.

Joseph John Bowman

Frail children of dust
And feeble as frail,
In Thee do we trust
Nor find Thee to fail.
Thy mercies, how tender,
How firm to the end,
Our Maker, Defender,
Redeemer, and Friend!

O measureless Might,
Ineffable Love,
While angels delight
To hymn Thee above,
Thy humbler creation,
Though feeble their lays,
With true adoration
Shall sing to Thy praise.

Robert Grant

CHAPTER TWO –
SEPARATION OF THE NAZARITES

Before getting into the passage, we will spend the most time with; let us look at some of God's plans for the separation of His people. The first point is in Numbers 6 and is the separation of the Nazarite. To get the whole picture that God planned for these individuals, read the entire chapter. It is very informative that the vow of the Nazarite was not for only one group of people or one tribe. It was not only for one sex. All were encouraged to take part in it.

God identified those who could take part in this work by saying,

> "When either man or woman shall separate themselves
> unto the Lord" (Num. 6:2).

The first and most vital part of any separation must be "Unto the Lord." If it is not unto Him, any separation from the things of this world will only be a ritual, and will not be pleasing to God in any way. God desired that His people separate themselves unto Him in this manner. He is not forcing them to do it but was leaving it unto their own free choice. His desire and plan are that we live separated lives. Despite that, He will never force us to do so.

Not only is separation to be unto the Lord, it is to be from all that God hates in this wicked world. There is nothing about this world and its systems in which God finds pleasure. We may dabble in them. However, they in no way, bring any joy to the heart of God. He will never bless us in our worldly enterprises. While that truth is acknowledged, many believers will succeed physically and financially in this world. They may advance socially and in every other manner.

9

Joseph John Bowman

These are the words of the Psalmist as he looked back at the ways God had blessed His people after He delivered them from the Land of Egypt.

> "They soon forgot His works; they waited not for His counsel: but lusted exceedingly in the wilderness, and tempted God in the desert. And He gave them their request; but sent leanness into their soul" (Ps. 106:13-15).

May the above never be said concerning any child of God. that they were so driven and desired the things of this world so much that their spiritual lives were put on hold. As a result, the God they served and who died for their salvation was required to send a spiritual leanness into their souls, even though they may be experiencing much blessing and advancement in this world. Worldly blessing in no way is indicative of the blessing of God. Conversely, it is not an indication of the punishment of God on a Saint.

He may chastise or punish us if our lives are in fellowship with the world and not unto Him. The fact that we experience the discipline is evidence that we are the children of God.

> "For whom the Lord loveth He chasteneth, and scourgeth every son whom He receiveth. If ye endure chastening, God dealeth with you as with sons: for what son is he whom the Father chasteneth not? But if ye be without chastisement, whereof all are partakers, then are ye bastards, and not sons" (Heb. 12:6-8).

If we live the lives of this world, we can expect God's hand in judgment to fall. It is noticeable that this is not the judgment that will come upon this world. That is the judgment of a judge condemning a criminal. However, the judgment we are experiencing is the punishment of a parent against an erring child. It can be expected from our loving Father. He places us under His hand. We are to yield to it, and, become more like Christ as a result of His work in us.

Separation from the World

John tells us;

> "For all that is in the world, the lust of the flesh, and the lust of the eyes, and the pride of life, is not of the Father, but is of the world" (1 John 2:16).

These three areas sum up everything that humanity finds pleasing in this world, and God tells us that there is nothing in this wicked old world, pleasing though it may be. No aspect of this world comes from Him. Therefore, we are to separate ourselves from it.

The following hymn tells of what we have left behind.

I've Turned my Back upon the World

I've turned my back upon the world
With all its idle pleasures,
And set my heart on better things,
On higher, holier treasures;
No more its glitter and its glare,
And vanity shall blind me;
I've crossed the separating line,
And left the world behind me.

Far, far behind me!
Far, far behind me!
I've crossed the separating line,
And left the world behind me.

I've left the old sad life of sin,
Its follies all forsaken;
My standing place is now in Christ,
His holy vows I've taken;
Beneath the standard of the cross
The world henceforth shall find me;
I've passed in Christ from death to life,

Joseph John Bowman

And left the world behind me.
Far, far behind me!
Far, far behind me!
I've passed in Christ from death to life,
And left the world behind me.

My soul shall ne'er return again
Back to its former station
For here alone is perfect peace,
And rest from condemnation;
I've made exchange of masters now,
The vows of glory bind me,
And once for all I've left the world,
Yes, left the world behind me.

Far, far behind me!
Far, far behind me!
And once for all I've left the world,
Yes, left the world behind me.

My choice is made forevermore,
I want no other Saviour;
I ask no purer happiness
Than His sweet love and favor;
My heart is fixed on Jesus Christ,
No more the world shall blind me;
I've crossed the Red Sea of His death,
And left the world behind me.

Far, far behind me!
Far, far behind me!
I've crossed the Red Sea of His death,
And left the world behind me.

Elisha A. Hoffman

Separation from the World

1. Separation of the Nazarite – Unto the Lord

Separation of the believer was to be first, unto the Lord. Only then was it to be from certain activities and relationships.

Before starting with the next section, let us look at what led up to the individual, making the vow of the Nazarite. Although what will follow was all an essential part of his vow, it did not constitute the main reason for the existence of the vow. Read the following verse carefully. It will be plain what the crucial point was that caused this event to take place.

> "And the Lord spake unto Moses, saying, speak unto the children of Israel, and say unto them, when either man or women shall separate themselves to vow a vow of a Nazarite, to separate themselves unto the Lord" (Num. 6:2).

The people of God were called to separate themselves unto a unique aspect of separation. If any believer has not separated themselves initially unto the Lord, any other aspect of separation is not possible to attain. Failure on behalf of a believer may limit their activities in some areas. As well there may be physical problems and aspects that will cause problems and deficiencies in the life and service of a believer. Despite these limitations, every believer can separate themselves unto the Lord. Any other type of separation is only an outward form if a God-ward separation has not preceded it. Each of us needs to be aware of the importance to whom it is we are separated. We not separated unto any function or work. It is not an organization or group or alliance unto whom we are separated. Initially, our separation is to be unto the God we serve. Otherwise, any separation in which we are engaged in is ineffectual and unsatisfactory before God. Every one of us needs to acknowledge this in our lives to come into a place of acceptance before Him. If we expect our service to be accepted in His sight, it must be based on an acceptable basis. The only way for that to happen is for its aim to be on Him who is our Lord and God.

13

Joseph John Bowman

i) Separation unto our Salvation

Every believer, no matter who they are, and what their spiritual standing can experience separation unto the Lord. It begins with the salvation of our souls. At that time, we will experience the only real rest available. It is through the work of the Lord Jesus on the cross.

He offers it free to all who would take of its benefits.

> "Come unto Me, all ye that labor and are heavy laden, and I will give you rest. Take My yoke upon you, and learn of Me; for I am meek and lowly in heart, and ye shall find rest unto your souls. For My yoke is easy, and My burden is light" (Matt. 11:28-10).

He is the only One who can save us and give us rest. The only way to receive that rest is to come unto Him. For our salvation, we must be separated unto Him to receive the value of the work He has available for us. At the same time we are saved we need to acknowledge who He is personally. Paul told us that for our salvation to be accomplised need to recognize who He is who saves us.

God said about His ability to save us,

> "I am the way, the truth, and the life: no man cometh unto the Father but by Me" (John 14:6).

Unless He is given His rightful place, salvation will not be accomplished. We have this truth emphasized in this Scripture.

> "That if thou shalt confess with thy mouth the Lord Jesus, and shalt believe in thine heart that God hath raised Him from the dead, thou shalt be saved" (Rom. 10:9).

Another rendering of this verse goes,

> "Because, if you confess with your mouth that Jesus is
> Lord and believe in your heart that God has raised Him
> from the dead, you will be saved" (Rom. 10:9 RSV).

We must acknowledge that He is Lord, that He is the One who is
overall to submit to Him as our Saviour if we are going to accept that
He has the power and authority to save us from our sins.

ii) Separating to Worship Him

We, as believers, are exhorted to worship the One who has saved us.
Peter tells us of our responsibility to worship Him. It is because of
the marvelous position into which He has brought us.

> "But ye are a chosen generation, a royal priesthood,
> an holy nation, a peculiar people: that ye should show
> forth the praises of Him who hath called you out of
> darkness unto His marvelous light" (1 Pet. 2:9).

As we do, we are to remember the greatness of the price paid for our
redemption. The Psalmist said,

> "Gather My Saints together unto Me; those that have
> made a covenant with Me by sacrifice" (Pas. 50:5).

We are to gather out of this world unto His name to worship Him for
all that He has done for us. We have no other choice offered unto us.

iii) Separating to His Authority

In light of this subject, we have the verse given to us by our Lord.
He looked ahead into time and saw the possible situations that would
develop among His people and the disagreements and dissensions

Joseph John Bowman

that would come among them; He gave this verse. In it, we have the solution to all our problems.

> "For where two or three are gathered together in My
> name, there am I in the midst of them" (Matt. 18:20).

If we remember that He is in our midst and that He is the One we are gathered around, it will make any problems seem inconsequential. He is to be our Guide and the One who is our Director. He is the One we are to follow. Any decisions we make are to be with His guidance and direction in view. As such, we will no longer be working towards our interests. Our self-absorbed desires will now take second place.

Paul told the Philippian believers,

> "Let nothing be done through strife and vain glory:
> but in lowliness of mind, let each esteem other better
> than themselves" (Phil. 2:3).

If we are striving with our brethren, we are seeking to put them down. When we are exhibiting vainglory, we are putting ourselves up. Both are wrong.

Our desire should be to acknowledge Him as,

> "King of kings and Lord of lords" (Re. 19:16).

When we do, we will have no trouble bowing to His authority. It is to be seen in our lives both individually as well as corporately.

iv) Separation in our Service

Many verses and passages in our Bible exhort us to live separate lives in our service to Him. I will only give a few at this time.

> "I beseech you therefore, brethren, by the mercies of
> God, that ye present your bodies a living sacrifice,

holy, acceptable unto God, which is your reasonable service. And be not conformed to this world: but be ye transformed by the renewing of your mind, that ye may prove what is that good, and acceptable, and perfect, will of God" (Rom 12:1-2).

Sacrifices have no will of their own. They cannot act independently of the will of the one to whom it is offered. It cannot rebel against the actions of the one who is offering them. The offering spoken of in these verses has voluntarily given itself to the One spoken. In all their actions and work, they are under the power of He who is their Lord. The life described is such that it is now a credit to the God of Heaven. In all things, the offering is separated unto God.

The apostle Paul was speaking about the value and responsibility of one whose life was serving God.

As he looked upon them, he made this observation.

"Let a man so account of us, as of the ministers (or servants – Ed.) of Christ, and stewards of the mysteries of God. Moreover, it is required in stewards, that a man be found faithful (1 Cor. 4:1-2).

I can remember my father saying that he was so glad that verse two did not end by saying that the requirement for a steward was that they are successful. Success is a relative term, depending on who is viewing its actions. God is not looking for us to be successful. All success is dependent on Him and the blessings He gives. Our duty and responsibility to be found faithful. Only then will He bless us and the work He has entrusted us to do. In all that we do, let us live lives of separation unto Him, as we serve the best of Masters.

Joseph John Bowman

v) Matrimonial Separation

The next is probably one of the most vital in the lives of individual believers. Sadly, it is also the one that is the most often broken and ignored. The teaching is that there is to be no marriage union between a saved and unsaved partner. There is no possibility of compromise or any other interpretation of this prohibition. It is taught right from the beginning of our Bible to the end.

It is in one of the most explicit passages on this subject in the New Testament.

> "Be not unequally yoked (or joined – Ed.) together with unbelievers: for what fellowship hath righteousness with unrighteousness? And what communion hath light with darkness? And what concord hath Christ with Belial? Or what part hath he that believeth with an infidel? And what agreement hath the temple of God with idols? For ye are the Temple of the living God, and they shall be My people. Wherefore come out from among them, and be ye separate, saith the Lord, and touch not the unclean thing: and I will receive you. And will be a Father unto you, and ye shall be My sons and daughters, saith the Lord Almighty" (2 Cor. 6:14-18).

While there are different areas of separation spoken of in these verses, the teaching is clear. Union of believers with unbelievers is forbidden. Under no circumstances was it to be countenanced or allowed. God judged the Nation of Israel for mixing and losing their separation on numerous occasions in the Old Testament. He refused to allow His holiness to be defiled by infringement with the godless world around. In like manner, we, as believers, are under an injunction to live separate lives now. In no area is this more important than in the marriage union. It will affect not only the individual lives of the believers involved but the lives of the local Churches in which they fellowship. Almost more importantly, it will have an adverse reaction

Separation from the World

and influence on the lives of any children born into that family. Be very careful before entering any union with the world. Be especially careful before entering into a marriage union with an unsaved person. God has condemned any union of this type. Moving in this way will be in direct disobedience to the will and Word of God. You cannot expect the blessing of God to follow.

vi) Separation in our Private Lives

There is no part of the life of a believer that is to be held separate from the guiding hand of God. In everything, we are under His divine hand.

Peter sums up the manner of lives we are to live before God.

> "As obedient children, not fashioning yourselves according to the former lusts in your ignorance: but as He which hath called you is holy, so be ye holy in all manner of conversation (manner of lifestyles – Ed.): because it is written, Be ye holy: for I am holy" (1 Pet. 1:14-16).

We sometimes shy away from any relationship with the word holy or holiness. In its purest form, it means a life that is without any stain upon it. It tells us that it is a life separated unto the Lord. In all that we do, we are now living lives that are separated from this wicked world and dedicated unto the God who saved us. It tells us that we have now changed masters and that the manner of our lives is different. We now have different goals and aims in our lives than we did before. We are now looking forward to a different Home than we did in times past. We are now called Saints. We were sinners and enemies of God; now, we are heirs and joint-heirs with Jesus Christ. All of this and more is wrapped up in the thought that we are now made holy through our salvation. As a result, we should be living holy lives before Him.

As a result of our new position before Him, we are now,

Joseph John Bowman

"Called out of darkness unto His marvelous light"
(1 Pet. 2:9).

We are the children of God and can call God our Father.

Paul said to the believers in Philippi:

"That ye may be blameless and harmless, the sons of
God, without rebuke, in the midst of a crooked and
perverse nation, among whom ye shine as lights in the
world" (Phil. 2:15).

vii)   Separation in our Prayers

Our prayers should not bear any resemblance to those of the world
around us.

The Lord Jesus said,

"But when ye pray, use not vain repetitions, as the
heathen do: for they think that they shall be heard for
their much speaking" (Matt. 6:7).

When we pray, it is not the number of words we use or the number of
subjects that we cover that count. It is all summed up in the following
verses.

The Lord Jesus, who knew how to pray acceptably said;

"After this manner, therefore, pray ye: Our Father
which art in Heaven, hallowed be Thy name. Thy
kingdom come. Thy will be done in earth as it is in
Heaven. Give us this day our daily bread. And forgive
us our debts, as we forgive our debtors. And lead us
not into temptation, but deliver us from evil: for Thine
is the kingdom and the power, and the glory, forever,
Amen" (Matt. 6:9-13).

Separation from the World

We are under no exhortation to pray this prayer specifically. Alternatively we are nowhere commanded to repeat it verbatim. I can recall, as a child in school repeating this prayer, daily, before the start of every school day. A short reading from the Bible usually followed it. There was nothing wrong with that. It instilled in the student's respect and acknowledgment of the God of Heaven. We developed a reverence and respect for who He is and was. All of that is lacking in many schools and among the population in general today.

It is not the quoting of a few words, no matter how important they may be. We can do that by rote and not realize the importance of the words we are saying. It is the acknowledgment and reception of the truths laid out in these verses that we need to learn.

Prayer starts with the knowledge that God is our Father. The truth that Heaven is His home and everything about His blessed person is holiness personified is. Following that, in all things, we are to bow to His will everywhere. It is not only in Heaven but on the earth, and in every aspect of our activities. We are then to thank God for the earthly blessings He has given us. As we do, we are to acknowledge the fact that we have sinned and ask God for His forgiveness. At the same time, we are asking God to forgive our sins; we are to forgive anyone who may have sinned against us. It matters not whether they have asked for our forgiveness. We are to forgive them first, and any responsibility to ask our forgiveness is on them and not on us. We are to ask God to preserve us from evil in all its various forms. In the end, we are to recognize that the God to whom we are coming is the One who rules not only in Heaven, but on earth, and in the universe around us.

In all we do, as we come before Him, we do so in the full knowledge that He is that One who is supreme. There is none like Him on earth or in Heaven. Coming before Him in prayer, we are doing so in the knowledge of His greatness, and the opportunity that is given us. We end by acknowledging the greatness of who He is, and that all might and power reside with Him. We close by giving an amen to

Joseph John Bowman

our prayer. We acknowledge that in everything we have prayed that God is overall.

In everything we have prayed and the contents of our prayers, we are in no ways like unto the world around us. Our prayers in no way legitimize who we are or raise us into a position of greatness or might. Instead, we are worshipping Him who is over all and above all, who is blessed forever and ever. He is the one to whom all praise is due and to whom we are coming as purged worshippers.

viii)   Separation in our Sorrows

It is crucial for every believer to recognize that their sorrows and sufferings are not the same as those of the world. The truth of this comes before us after the death of the Lord Jesus. On the evening of the third day, there was a couple who were walking from Jerusalem home. As they walked, they were discussing the things that had happened around the crucifixion of the Lord Jesus.

We read these words,

> "And it came to pass, that, while they communed together and reasoned, Jesus Himself drew near, and went with them" (Luke 24:15).

It is vital for every believer to realize that in all our sufferings, and sorrows, our Lord is there with us.

At this point, I want to give the words of the following servants of God.

> "Knots on the root of the oak tree tell of many storms
> And how deep the roots have forced their way into the earth.
> Thus the Christian is made strong and firmly
> rooted by the storms of life."

Charles Spurgeon.

Separation from the World

A verse from an unknown poet said,

"There is a reason a glorious reason
For everything, the Lord may send your way –
When there's nothing going right,
Walk by faith, and not by sight –
There's a reason, so rejoice the livelong day."

Anonymous

A hymn written years ago tells us the plan of God for our lives.

"Through Fiery Trials with God"

"What shall I learn from God
Through fiery trials today.
As side by side He walks with me
Along life's rugged way?
He never fails – not even
In the darkest hour.
I know my Lord is nigh –
I feel His power.

Today I thank Him
For His love and grace.
In perfect peace, the future
I can face.
He knows of each new need
Before "The Day"
And lovingly my Saviour
Plans my earthly way.

As day by day I feed
Upon God's Word,
I learn my step is "ordered
Of the Lord."

Joseph John Bowman

So also every stop in just
Another step to test,
And prove to me one fact –
God's way is always best.

I only want whatever
God has planned.
So all is well, He holds me
In His hand.
So I can trust Him now
To lead aright,
As I walk on with Him
Through faith – not sight.

Then through this fiery trial
What doth my Saviour say?
Perhaps just this, be still
My child, lean hard and pray.
Today I learned anew to answer.
"Lord Thy way is best"
Now help me to be still –
Lean hard – and pray and rest."

Author Unknown

I will end these quotations with a word from a dear sister in the Lord.

"The Lord is faithful; it is not so much for us to understand as to trust" (Elizabeth Funston).

"Trust in the Lord with all thine heart, and lean not unto thine own understanding. In all thy ways acknowledge Him, and He shall direct thy paths" (Prov. 3:5-6).

Paul told us concerning the passing in death of fellow believers,

Separation from the World

"But I would not have you to be ignorant, brethren, concerning them which are asleep, that ye sorrow not, even as others which have no hope…..Wherefore, comfort one another with these words" (1 Thess. 4:13 & 18).

Every believer has a hope beyond the grave. It is that we will one day be at home with the Lord. We will all be with the Lord, but we will all be together in that glorious place. There is much in our Bibles to tell us of the wonders of the home to which we are going. It is a hope, unlike anything this world has to offer. The apostle Paul tells us that there was a time when he was caught up into Heaven.

He seeks to describe it in this way.

"How that he (Paul – Ed.) was caught up into Paradise (Heaven – Ed.), and heard unspeakable words, which it is not lawful for a man to utter" (2 Cor. 12:4).

The apostle Paul sums up both the present experiences as well as the future hope of every believer in the following words.

"For we know that if our earthly house of this tabernacle were dissolved, we have a building of God, an house not made with hands, eternal in the Heavens. (Cor. 5:1).

It is the hope of every believer. It is what makes our sufferings, and sorrows bearable. It is what makes us separate people. It puts us apart from the hopelessness and sorrows of the world around us. We rejoice in that blessed hope. One day all the trials and sorrows or this earth will be passed.

Speaking of the passing effects of our trials we are told,

"For our light affliction which is but for a moment, worketh for us a far more exceeding and eternal weight of glory" (2 Cor. 4:17).

Joseph John Bowman

A dear sister (Anne Chung) once said that her favorite verse in the Bible was

"And it came to pass."

She explained that it all came to pass; it did not come to stay. May we take comfort in the transitory nature of the trials come upon each one of us.

We have an eternal hope. We can live in light of it. For it is not just a hope that is dependent on a lucky chance. It is dependent on an absolute and secure fact. It rests on the promise of God and the work of our Lord Jesus Christ. Because of that, we know that all our sorrows will be over one day. We will then dwell forever in the presence of God. We will ever be with Him in all His glories. As we contemplate what lies ahead, the sorrows and pains of this earth are but inconsequential at the most.

2. Separation of the Nazarite – Worldly Joys

From Moses writings,

"He shall separate himself from wine and strong drink, and shall drink no vinegar of wine, or vinegar of strong drink, neither shall he drink any liquor of grapes, nor eat moist grapes, or dried. All the days of his separation shall he eat nothing that is made of the vine tree, from the kernels even to the husk" (Num. 6:3-4.).

Wine and the fruit of the vine speak to us of joy in the Bible. Sometimes it is the joys of the Spirit and the things of God. On other occasions, it speaks of the joys of this world. In this passage, it tells us of joys that come from this world. Not everything associated with the grape and its joys was forbidden to the child of God. However, if one was to live a life of separation unto God and to His things, these joys were to be put to one side. The only source of joy for a godly

26

man or women was to be that found in the things of God. It was a prohibition that did not apply to everyone. If a separated individual was to live by their vow of separation, it must apply in every way.

He was not to engage in anything influenced by this world's joys. Joy, either divine or human, is what wine speaks of in Scripture. The joys of this life, legitimate as they might be for some of the people of God, were "Anathema" (accursed) for him. There is that in this world that brings temporary joy to the heart of man. They may seem to be all right. However, God desires that the man or woman who truly seeks to follow Him abstain from them. The joys of this earth are only fleeting. They are only for a season.

I recently bought a new car. It is a year later, and it is now old. There are options for new cars that were not available last year. We all desire that which is new. Every manufacturer and business depends on this fact. We are encouraged to be perpetually dissatisfied with whatever it is we have. That is how every business maintains its sales quotas and makes its profits. Although I was happy in the past, now I am dissatisfied. The same is said about all the joys this world has to offer. They may bring us joy and happiness for a moment, but it will pass. When we come to joy, which is from God, and this world's happiness, we can say the following.

> "Joy is the result of a sure reliance on an established fact; happiness is dependant on the circumstances that surround us."

As a result, no believer should ever lose joy given by God. Even a small change in circumstances can cause anyone to lose happiness that comes from this world. Let us make sure that we are secure in the joy derived from our salvation. The world only offers fleeting joys.

Not only will they not last in time, but they will all cease and disappear in eternity. There will only be everlasting joy and peace among the people of God from the throne of God. We should seek, as believers, to live in that joy every day.

Joseph John Bowman

Well might the hymn writer say:

Oh Christ in Thee my Soul hath Found

"Oh Christ, in Thee my soul hath found
And found in Thee alone,
The peace, the joy, I sought so long,
The bliss till now unknown.

Chorus

Now, none but Christ can satisfy,
None other name for me!
There's love and life and lasting joy,
Lord Jesus found in Thee!

I sighed for rest and happiness,
I yearned for them, not Thee;
But while I passed my Saviour by,
His love laid hold on me.

I tried the broken cisterns, Lord,
But, ah! The waters failed!
E'en as I stooped to drink they fled
And mocked me as I wailed.

The pleasures lost I sadly mourned,
But never wept for Thee,
Till grace the sightless eyes received,
Thy loveliness to see."

Anonymous

The joys of this earth can bring the believer no long-term satisfaction. Indeed, they can bring no short-term satisfaction. The only joy, peace, and satisfaction the believer can find are in the person of the Lord Jesus Christ.

Separation from the World

Peter told us so clearly,

> "Whom having not seen ye love; in whom though now ye see Him not, yet believing, ye rejoice with joy unspeakable and full of glory" (1 Pet.1:8).

Our love for Him brings out the joy that resides in our hearts. Peter tells us that it is an indescribable joy. He calls it unspeakable. It is the only time this Greek word is in the New Testament. His love for us is so unique that there is no other word to describe the joy He gives us. We cannot begin to describe in words how incredible the joy and peace are which we have in Him. Our joy rests in our knowledge of Him. It is available to each one of us if we will take advantage of it.

(Note: This is joy and not happiness. Happiness is affected by the situations in which we find ourselves. If those situations change our happiness and all that goes along with it can depart. Joy comes from within and is independent of outward circumstances or influences. We can, and do, experience joy that comes from God. It is evident in the midst of the most adverse circumstances. The one is altogether independent of the other.)

Paul says,

> "But the fruit of the Spirit is love, JOY, peace, longsuffering, gentleness, goodness, faith, meekness, temperance, against such there is no law. (Gal. 5:22-23).

Joy is something that should be characteristic of every believer. We should experience it apart from the joys of this life. Indeed, we should not partake of this world's joys expecting that they will supplement the joys that we get from God. They will take away from the God-given joys in which God wants us to dwell. These joys come from two different sources. Consequently, they should have nothing to do with each other.

Joseph John Bowman

3. Separation of the Nazarite – Earthly Shame

The second area of separation is that;

> "All the days of the vow of his separation there shall no
> razor come upon his head: until the days be fulfilled,
> in the which he separateth himself unto the Lord, he
> shall be holy, and shall let the locks of the hair of his
> head grow." (Numb. 6:5).

Paul speaks of God's estimation of a man's long hair.

> "Doth not even nature itself (or the nature of it – Ed.)
> teach you that, if a man have long hair, it is a shame
> unto him?" (1 Cor. 11:14).

The apostle tells us in this verse, a man's long hair was his shame.
Unfortunately, some Christian brethren have let their hair grow long
today. They seem to believe that what God called their shame is now
an emblem of pride. They use it as a means of identification. Some
believers seem to want to rebel against what has been called the
establishment. They think by letting their hair grow long; they are
making a statement on their individuality. The thought is that if it was
taught and practiced by believers in past eras, it is wrong. Therefore,
it must be discarded as irrelevant for the society of Christians today.
Many are seeking to rewrite the Bible. By so doing, they are deleting
whole portions of the Scriptures of Truth. They are eliminating truths
taught and held fervently for generations. Their thought is that God
will recognize their desire and honor them for their wish to serve Him.

In it all and through it all, we have the words of Samuel to King Saul.

> "Behold, to obey is better than sacrifice, and to
> hearken than the fat of rams" (1 Sam. 15:22).

What a shame that this action has found a place amidst God's people!

Separation from the World

I will quote the verse dealing with God's condemnation of a man having long hair again.

> "Doth not even nature itself teach you, that if a man have long hair, it is a shame unto him" (1 Cor. 11:14).

The word "Nature" in this verse means

> "Growth by germination or expansion, natural production."

It is telling us that it is natural for an animal to act in a certain way in the wild. In nature, it is one of the means of continuing existence. Most males will show off their beauty and wonders. Look at many male animals in their natural habitats. They are seen exhibiting the beauty and strength of nature. They portray all that God gave them. That function is the natural action found in nature.

It is to be different among the people of God. We are not to be seen exhibiting our glories for all to see. That is not the position God desires for us. God has brought this picture before us in the short hair of the man and the covered long hair of the woman.

Verse 15 tells us that long hair is glory, or source of boasting, to the woman. Her long hair shows God the glory of the man. When He sees it, God views not only the glory of man but the glory of His Son. However, verse 14 is telling us that this glory is to be cut. The reason is, man is the visible representation of the glory of God on earth. It is the glory of God that is seen through man and not his glories.

In the same way, the glories of God shine forth through the submission of the sisters to the Word of God. Submission never implies subservience. By showing forth her submission, the sister is telling both the Saints, as well as the world that she is living her life in submission to her Lord.

When believers act in this way, we have the words of Peter.

31

Joseph John Bowman

> "Unto whom it was revealed, that not unto themselves, but unto us that did minister (serve in – Ed.) the things, which are now reported unto you by them that have preached the gospel unto you with the Holy Ghost sent down from Heaven; which things the angels desire to look into" (1 Pet. 1:12).

Paul said about the privileged position a sister has in the local gathering;

> "For this cause ought the woman to have power on her head (or a sign of the power or authority she is now under – Ed.) because of the angels" (1 Cor. 11:10).

Paul looked at the heights and privileges given to angels. The wonder we are dealing with is that great though angels are, they are looking in wonder on our obedience. Through viewing our Godly actions, they worship the God whom they serve. It shows the place of authority we have entered. Angels view the place of responsibility that we, as believers, have been brought through grace.

Paul said, looking upon every Saint in their strengths and weaknesses:

> "Know ye not that we (the Saints of God – Ed.) shall judge angels? How much more to the things that pertain to life? (1 Cor. 6:3).

(In this verse the Saints are given authority to judge the affairs of the people of God. We are forbidden to go to the courts of this land for any action against another believer. Judgment is through the decisions of God's people.)

Since the above verses are accurate, and beyond dispute, how dare any of us to act in such a way that will bring dishonor unto the name of Christ. Our desire should be to act so that His glories will shine forth. It should make them more evident to all around.

Separation from the World

The question dealing with short hair in the brethren is,

"Does nature teach this in any other way?"

We found the answer in Psalm 19:1-6. He starts with his exclamation in verse 1.

"The heavens declare the glory of God: and the firmament showeth His handiwork" (Ps. 19:1).

If nature shows forth the glory of God, how dare any man have the impunity to act in a way that will disgrace His holy name?

Long hair was a shame for the man in the Old Testament as well. The principles of God have never changed. What displeased God in one era continued into the next. In like manner, what He found shameful in one Dispensation was equally shameful in the ones that preceded it.

In Numbers 6, the Nazarite was bearing shame for the person of God. In this way, his testimony shone forth before all.

He was identifying himself with that One Whom men despised.

"He is despised and rejected of men: a man of sorrows, and acquainted with grief: and we hid as it were our faces from Him: He was despised, and we esteemed Him not" (Is. 53:3).

The writer to the Hebrew laid Him before us as our example.

"Wherefore Jesus also, that He might sanctify the people with His own blood, suffered without the gate. Let us go forth therefore unto Him without the camp, bearing His reproach" (Heb. 13:12-13).

With this example before us, we should not hesitate to bear shame for His blessed name. Any shame we bear, we should count as a privilege.

Joseph John Bowman

We are not to count it as a burden to bear, or as a hardship. He bore all for us. Why should we shrink from bearing shame for Him?

We do not have examples of individuals in this passage, doing things that displeased God in order to honor Him. By obeying the rules, God laid down for a person to become a Nazarite, they agreed with God. They are acknowledging by abstaining from these three things that by taking part in them was wrong. While these items may not be wrong for most people, they were for them, that is because they have set themselves apart for the service of God. By so doing they have publicly stated they are separate from all the things of this world. God will honor those who live in this manner.

(As a note here, the days of an individual physically taking the oath of the Nazarite with all that pertains to it is passed. The physical actions in the Old Testament are now spiritually seen in the pictures they present to us.)

Shame is an aspect of the Christian life we have all been called to suffer. The early believers, after they had been arrested and beaten, were commanded that they speak not in the name of Jesus.

Their immediate response was,

> "And they departed from the presence of the council, (Sanhedrim – Ed.) rejoicing that they were counted worthy to suffer shame for His name" (Acts 5:41).

When we suffer shame for the name of our Lord, do we rejoice? Do we receive it grudgingly or do we accept it joyfully, as those whom the Lord has counted worthy to suffer for His name? Is the reason we suffer so little because we are not worthy?

The early disciples rejoiced throughout their time of persecution.

> "They ceased not to teach and preach (Evangelize) Jesus Christ" (Acts 5:42).

Separation from the World

The shame which we suffer, or do not suffer, is brought into stark contrast with all that our Lord went through.

> "Looking unto Jesus the Author and Finisher of (our) faith" (Heb. 12:2).

(Leave out the pronoun "Our." He is the Captain or Leader, and Perfector of "Faith," not "Our faith." It is the entire body of faith itself of which He is the Leader. Our faith makes us a small part of the whole.)

> "Who for the joy that was set before Him, endured the cross, despising the shame, and is set down at the right hand of the throne of God" (Heb. 12:2).

The shame He suffered at the hands of man comes before us in Isaiah 53:2-3. Humanity despised and rejected Him; they blasphemed His holy name. His trial, before His crucifixion, was marked by their hatred.

They

> "Spake all manner of evil against Him falsely" (Matt. 25:60).

John told us

> "He came unto his own (Things – Ed.) and His own (People – Ed.) received Him not" (John 1:11).

The real world that He had created was where He came. Incredibly, His own chosen people rejected Him. At His birth, they sought to put Him to death. They sought occasion against Him, to put Him to death. They found false witnesses to witness against Him, and even their witnesses agreed not (Mark 14:56). In Luke 23:8-12, Herod's men of war treated Him abominably.

Joseph John Bowman

They

> "Set Him at naught" (Luke 23:11).

These words tell us that they made Him walk through a cordon of soldiers. He walked by while they hit Him and beat Him and spit upon Him. They treated Him shamefully as if He was beneath contempt as far as they were concerned. They showed the how much they despised His blessed Person and work. They did their utmost to show the level of contempt they had for the Son of God.

The words "Set at naught" mean

> "To make nothing utterly of, to despise."

The Greek word tells us of hatred and scorn that they had for the Son of God. Herod's men-of-war treated Him as if He was of absolutely no value. In their treatment of Him, they showed their lack of respect.

They,

> "Mocked Him, and arrayed Him in a gorgeous robe" (Luke 23:11).

They blasphemed His holy name and made a mockery of His claim to be the King of the Jews. They mocked His Holy Person as One that was contemptible, and only worth their ridicule and scorn. They laughed at Him and made light of who He was and why He came.

The Roman soldiers under Pilate

> "Clothed Him with purple, and platted a crown of thorns, and put it upon His head, and began to salute Him, Hail, King of the Jews! And they smote Him with a reed and did spit upon Him and bowing their knees worshipped Him" (Mark 15:17-19).

36

Separation from the World

(The spitting in the face (also Matthew 26:27) was the most humiliating action performed upon another human being. It shows the totality of their contempt for Him. To insult someone, you spit at their feet, never on them and certainly never in their face. I recently had an acquaintance who was from that part of the world, state that no matter what you thought of a person, you never spit on them. As an indication of your derision, you would spit at their feet but never on them, and certainly never in their face.)

The treatment of our blessed Lord Jesus Christ was viler than we can ever imagine. It showed the contempt in which they held Him. They considered Him less than nothing. In their consideration, there was no one more contemptible or whom they abhorred more. The question must be asked, "Is man any different today?" We may, or may not, be more sophisticated and civilized. We may be far better educated. Technologically we may be far more advanced. We may know more, but are we any better? Have we any more of a love for that One Who died for us? Try to witness for Him to someone in the world and see your reception. Humanity hates Him and would still put Him to death.

A newscaster recently said,

> "This world has only seen one perfect man and they
> put Him on a cross."

If that is their attitude why should we want to get into a relationship with them by trying to seek to influence the godless policies of this world, when they are the very ones who put Him to death?

We have contemplated some of the shame that our Lord went through to redeem us. We looked at the shameful way man treated the holy Son of God, without considering the punishment He endured at the hands of a holy God when He became the sin offering in our stead. That being the case, then why should we shrink from the thought of suffering shame for His blessed name? The Nazarite was commanded to let his hair grow all the days of his service to indicate to all around

Joseph John Bowman

him the shame; he was enduring. Even so, it should be with us. We are not to seek to lessen this shame by any amount of integration into the functions of this life that God has cursed; let alone by getting involved in the policies that govern it. That would disgrace our testimonies and shame the person of our Lord. It is a type of shame that would not bring glory to God. Sadly, it would cause His name to be reviled among the nations of this world.

4. Separation of the Nazarite – Purity

The third aspect of separation that we read of was regarding their purity.

The commandment was,

> "All the days that he separateth himself unto the Lord, he shall come at no dead body. He shall not make himself unclean for his father, or for his mother, for his brother, or for his sister, when they die: because the consecration of his God is upon his head. All the days of his separation, he is holy unto the Lord" (Num. 6:6-8).

They were to separate themselves from earthly joys and to suffer shame for God. The third point was a commandment from God against the touching of any dead body, regardless of who it may be. The commandment was that he is morally clean. He was not to come into any contact with the dead. A dead body always brings before us the results of sin.

James tells us,

> "Sin when it is finished, bringeth forth death" (James 1:15).

God places a very high premium on holiness.

He said,

> "But as He who called you is holy, so be ye holy in all manner of conversation; because it is written, 'Be ye holy; for I am holy'" (1Pet. 1:15-16).

God wants us to be holy in every manner of our lives. The example that He set forward for us to follow was not Peter, great though he was, for Peter failed. It was not Paul as the great apostle to the Gentiles, for Paul was a sinner. The example was One, who was without any failing or spot. It is Him we are to imitate. Every man no matter how great or spiritual, has their failings. No, He gave Himself as the Supreme Example. We know without a shadow of a doubt that God is holy. Holiness is to be in every aspect of our lives as we follow Him. Our lives should be such that they are a mirror through which the world can see Christ Jesus brought forth in us.

(Just a little note on what holiness is at this point. We often think of holiness as sinlessness, and it is. In everything a holy God is sinless. It is far more than that. It means to be separate. That tells us no matter what we may accomplish or achieve, God is separate from us. He lives in an entirely different realm and is untouched by the sins and deficiencies that we have. The holiness of God and that which comes from God tells us of His marvelous majesty. He rules the realms above. He is more significant and higher than all. He is that One who is beyond compare. All of these and more are brought before our gaze when we look at the word holy.

Although its meaning is so vast and far-reaching, yet God has made it attainable to His people. We are to live our lives as copies of Him, who is the Great Example. By so doing, we will be able to live lives of holiness before the Throne of God. In that, He will be satisfied. Our holy lives have nothing to do with our accomplishments or successes. Personal holiness is only attained through the work of His Son. In Him, God finds all His delight. We are to be holy because He is holy. It is not that we are to be holy as He is holy for this would be impossible. We can never, and will never, be as holy as God for Isaiah 57:15 tells us that

Joseph John Bowman

God inhabits eternity and that His very name is Holy. His is holiness that can never be touched or reached, but we can copy it.)

Moral purity is on several different levels. Paul is speaking to Timothy as he speaks about the man whose desire is to serve Him.

To be accepted and available in our service we must,

> "Flee also youthful lusts; but follow righteousness, faith, charity, peace, with them that call on the Lord out of a pure heart" (2 Tim.2:22).

We are commanded to flee any lusts that would negatively affect us. Now, in this passage, lust is an inordinate desire, or illegitimate longing, for something we do not possess or have any right to own. It is any longing or desire that puts God in second place.

It is covetousness.

> "For the love (lust or avarice, desire or coveteousness – Ed.) of money is the root of all evil" (1 Tim. 6:10).

These lusts and many others like them are available for the use of Satan and his demonic hosts. Satan has a whole arsenal of weapons at his disposal to war against the soul.

We read that those who so lusted have

> "Pierced themselves through with many sorrows" (1 Tim.6:10).

If we genuinely want to serve our Lord, we must follow His advice,

> "If a man (anyone – Ed.) therefore purges himself from these, he shall be a vessel unto honor, sanctified, and meet for the Master's use, prepared for every good work" (2 Tim. 2:21).

Separation from the World

Moral purity is essential if our service for God is going to be acceptable to Him whom we seek to please.

Purity is first in our relations with the opposite sex. (Or unfortunately, we need to mention those who engage in sexual activity with those of the same sex. What a disgrace it is to the very God of Heaven!) The point of the dreadfulness of this sin and God's estimation of it very clearly brought out in the following Scriptures (Read Leviticus 18:22, Romans 1:26-27). Voicing disagreement or disapproval will get you to be known as a troublemaker. Colleagues will shy away from you. Any impact previously had will be lost or stilted.

Scripture is unambiguous that any sexual relationship outside of the marriage bond is strictly prohibited. (It is a marriage between a man and a woman. It does not include the same-sex marriages found in society today.)

This teaching of moral purity is in the words of Paul.

> "Now concerning the things whereof ye wrote unto me; it is good for a man not to touch a woman" (1 Cor. 7:1).

The meaning of the verse is to touch carnally not casually.

The word "Touch" means

> "To attach oneself to (in many implied relations). Its root means "To fasten to, specifically to set on fire."

It is far more than a casual touch. It tells of touch with an implied meaning behind it. The thought is that it is to touch with carnal implications. It sets one, or both, of the participants on fire. Any thought of touching in this manner outside of marriage is strictly prohibited.

Joseph John Bowman

A safeguard for all believers is in the next verse.

> "Never-the-less, to avoid fornication (or because of fornication – Ed.) let every man have his own wife, and let every woman have her own husband" (1 Cor. 7:2).

(Fornication, though it includes adultery goes far beyond it. It includes every type of sexual uncleanness there is. This list goes on and on, and we hardly need in this society to list them. We do well not to use the two terms synonymously.) The sin, fornication, is so severe that in 1 Corinthians 5 it is included in the list of other sins for which a believer is excommunicated.

(The other sins listed are the covetous, the extortioner, the idolater, a drunkard, and a railer. As well, there are those who teach false doctrine in 1 Timothy 1:19-20 and those who cause division in Romans 16:17. There is also the individual in Matthew 18:15-19 who refuses reconciliation to a brother or sister seeking it.)

These sins are so severe that God will not allow one who commits them to continue in fellowship with His people. His holiness is such that they must be judged. These are extreme examples of moral impurity. There are many other types of sins that are not so extreme. We could go into all the different types of moral sins, but we will not for the sake of time. Suffice it to say a moral sin is one that hurts the character of a believer. The teaching for the Nazarite was that he is morally clean. He was to touch no dead body. He was to remain separate from any contact with the dead.

In Scripture, death always speaks of sin and its results.

This teaching in a straightforward manner explains the subject at hand. No area brings corruption forward more clearly than the political arena. The moral uncleanness of the participants is portrayed. Politicians are known for their dirty tricks and the outright deceptions and lies that they will utilize to get into power and stay there. Their desire to stay in power makes them even worse. There is a reason

Separation from the World

why the words politics and corruption are almost synonymous in our society. Even the citizenry of this world states; the two most despised professions are lawyers and politicians. They will do anything to win. Truth is a victim of their goals. It matters not what stands in their way. They will seek to do anything to those who undermine their ambitions.

There is a saying in the world that goes this way,

> "Power corrupts, and absolute power corrupts absolutely."

Even the world acknowledges that power corrupts those who engage in the political arena. Consequently, every believer should stay as far from it as possible. The truth includes voting for those who are running for their various offices. By so doing, we are identifying ourselves with the dirty tricks that they have used to get into office. Why should we seek to identify this lifestyle with a child of God? They should be those who desire to live a holy separated life. How can such a one work side by side with a godless unbeliever? That is not to say that some unbelievers do not have a high moral code. They may have great intentions. However, they are marred by sin.

In this place, I will give another Scripture,

> "Can two walk together, except they be agreed" (Amos 3:3).

In the Scriptures, the picture of walking together tells us that the participants were in fellowship with each other. Are the unsaved those we should be in close association with, in our daily walk?

We should view our example while we seek to decide which way to live. Will we follow him who is the Prince of the Power of the air or He of Whom the hymn writer is speaking?

Joseph John Bowman

Holy, Holy, Holy! Lord God Almighty!

Holy, Holy, Holy! Lord God Almighty!
Early in the morning, our song shall rise to Thee.
Holy, Holy, Holy! Merciful and Mighty!
God in three persons, blessed Trinty!

Holy, Holy, Holy! All the saints adore Thee,
Casting down their golden crowns around the glassy sea;
Cherubim and seraphim falling down before Thee,
Which wert and art and evermore shalt be.

Holy, Holy, Holy! Though the darkness hide Thee,
Though the eye made blind by sin Thy glory may not see,
Only Thou art holy; there is none beside Thee,
Perfect in pow'r, in love, and purity.

Holy, Holy, Holy! Lord God Almighty!
All Thy works shall praise Thy name on earth and sky and sea.
Holy, Holy, Holy! Merciful and Mighty!
God in three persons, blessed Trinty."
Reginald Heber

CHAPTER THREE –
SEPARATION OF ABRAHAM

I want to make a few comments on the separation that Abraham experienced before we deal with the present-day section in 2 Corinthians 6. The separation of Abraham is very instructive on some different fronts. Bear in mind, that while truths are presented, they are never unique to one passage. We find the same principles repeated time and time again. Seldom do we find the whole aspect of truth identified in one passage.

We need to compare Scripture with Scripture to find the totality of truth God is seeking to present to us.

> "For precept must be upon precept, precept upon precept; line upon line, line upon line; here a little, and there a little" (Is 28:10).

The truths of God are found the Scriptures. To find them, we need to look and search them out. Upon our study and diligence, God will display them to us.

The verse I want to look at is;

> "And the Lord said unto Abram, 'Get thee out of thy country, and from thy kindred, and from thy father's house, unto a land that I will show thee' (Gen. 12:1).

God is commanding Abraham to separate himself in some vitally essential areas. They are representative of truths brought before us

45

Joseph John Bowman

today. It does us well to remember that revelation continues and it grows in scope

Certain truths were made evident to Abraham. We today, have a much higher responsibility and a more complete revelation of the truth than Abraham.

The writer to the Hebrews was speaking about the completion of the truths in the Word of God. He recognized that truths and teachings in the Old Testament are incomplete as they are dealing with the new era they were now living. It was to be called the Church Age, or the Day of Grace. In it, believers would be guided by the complete Word of God, and no more needed to be added to it. Nothing was to be taken away from its pages.

It is complete.

> "For we know in part, and we prophecy in part. But when that which is perfect is come, then that which is in part shall be done away. When I was a child, I spake as a child. I understood as a child. I thought as a child: but when I became a man, I put away childish things. For, now we see through a glass, darkly: but then face to face: now I know in part: but then shall I know even as also I am known" (1 Cor. 13:9-12).

The first thing we must realize in our separation is what it is from and who it is to. First and foremost, for separation to be acceptable, it must be unto God. Then and only then, it is to be from the world.

Abraham's separation was unto God in that God had called him unto Himself. When God calls us,

we are to respond as Eli told Samuel when God called him.

> "Speak; for thy servant heareth" (1 Sam. 3:9).

Separation from the World

When called, our natural inclination should be to come. It was Abraham's response, seen in his unflinching obedience to the call. We nowhere read of Abraham questioning the wisdom of the call, for naturally speaking, it would have made no sense at all. He was leaving an important center of civilization to go to a place he had never seen. It was a place he had no conception of, and where he had never been. He did not even know where he was going, for God did not tell him where his destination was to be.

God only said that it was

"Unto a land that I will show thee" (Gen. 12:1).

However, he obeyed God and immediately separated himself unto the Lord. It should be our desire to seek to identify ourselves with that One who paid such a sublime price for us on Calvary.

Therefore,

"Let us go forth therefore unto Him without the camp bearing His reproach" (Heb.13:13).

Not only was Abram's separation unto God, but it was also from the world and all that it speaks of and represents. This world, which moves in direct rebellion to God, and defies Him to His face, is the enemy of God. As such, we should not become friends with it or be associated with it. I was thinking about that old hymn, "This World is a Wilderness Wide." The thought behind this hymn is very accurate. Darby clearly states what our priorities should be in his hymn.

This World is a Wilderness Wide

"This world is a wilderness wide
I have nothing to seek or to choose;
I've no tho't in the waste to abide:
I've naught to regret or to lose.

47

Joseph John Bowman

The path where my Savior is gone
Has led up to His Father and God
To the place where He's now on the throne,
And His strength shall be mine on the road.

'Tis treasure I've found in His love
That has made me a pilgrim below;
And 'tis there, when I reach Him above,
As I'm known, all His fullness I'll know."

J. N. Darby

1. Political Separation

The first point I want to look at in this context is Abraham's separation from his country. It tells us of political separation. A country, in those days, was a loose-knit amalgamation of city-states. Each city had its local government, which was responsible for its municipal decisions. They individually had kings or rulers who were independent of the kings who ruled the other city-states in the area. They made war against one another, and if victorious enslaved the inhabitants of the conquered city. They only would combine to work together if they had a common enemy who threatened them all. Ordinarily, they were in constant competition, the one with the other. The more powerful city-states were known for their great riches and the advances they made in the different medical, scientific, and technological fields. They were also known for their great wickedness and departure from God. That is the type of city from which Abraham came. An example in Genesis 19:1 is of the government of one of these cities.

The city was Sodom, and Lot, Abraham's nephew, sat in the gate. Lot's position showed the depths he had sunk in compromising the morals he had previously held. He now sat alongside those whose morals and ethics were such that soon, God was going to judge them. The judgment of God was to be so severe that from then onward, the very name of Sodom was to be synonymous with their sin. We are

48

Separation from the World

told emphatically of the hatred of God for their sinful lives. It only follows that a just God would judge sin. Even the heathen round about knew that God had moved against these cities and their sin.

The following Scripture shows us the wickedness of Sodom. It, also, tells us that although Lot had some moral scruples, they only went so far. The situation is dealing with the time when two angels of God entered the house of Lot. They were there to tell him that Sodom was to suffer destruction. Their purpose was to save Lot and his family from the annihilation God had planned for the city. Upon hearing of the arrival of these two men, the male citizens of Sodom stormed the house of Lot with this demand.

> "And they called unto Lot, and said unto him, where are the men which came into thee this night? Bring them out unto us, that we may know them (know them sexually – Ed.)" (Gen. 19:5).

Lot sought to resist the sinful urges of the men of the city. To seek to pacify them, he made the following offer.

> "Behold now, I have two daughters which have not known man: let me, I pray you, bring them out unto you, and do ye to them as is good in your eyes" (Gen. 19:8).

Instead of trusting the God of Abraham, he sank to the level of those around him. He offered his daughters to the men of the city to sexually abuse in any way they saw fit. The very fact that Lot was in that city was dishonoring to God. By his association with those around him, he absorbed the godless and wicked morals of the day. He did not approve of them. Unfortunately, when it was expedient, he was willing to work with them if it was advantageous to him. God found no pleasure in Lot being there. Lot, during his time among them, was unable to maintain a Godly testimony.

Joseph John Bowman

Fortunately, for Lot, God intervened and saved Lot and his daughters. The angels took Lot and his daughters out of the city to a place of safety. God moves in His sovereign way and might because He is sovereign. God is not limited to what He can do. He has all power to reach anyone and do anything because He is God. However, that does not give us the right to be in places or involved in activities that blaspheme the name of the Lord. Because God may turn what was evil and use it for good, does not justify our engaging in ungodly activities.

God saved Lot and his two daughters from the destruction of Sodom. However, his wife showed that her desire was with the residents of Sodom by looking back. For that, God judged her. Despite the dramatic way God moved to save them, Lots' daughters showed their immoral characters. It was enacted by their causing Lot to become the father of their children. They brought this shameful action into force by getting Lot drunk. He had no idea what was transpiring. However, it showed that even though they were out of Sodom, Sodom was not out of the girls. They maintained the desires and actions they had learned and seen during their time in Sodom. We need to be so careful that we do not negatively influence those who are younger into the things of this world. (That is younger in both a physical manner as well as those who are younger spiritually.)

The gate was where those who were responsible for the governmental decisions of the city sat. It was the equivalent of today's city council. It was a gathering of the high ranking dignitaries and leaders of the city. It included both those with political power as well as religious leaders. It also included those who sat as representatives of the local judicial system. In Genesis 19, Lot was involved in the governmental decisions of the city. The city was opposed to God by its actions and morals. Because of that, it eventually came under the judgment of God. In the judgment of God falling upon this city, we see an expression of His opinion. It is all encompassed by the statement about the position Lot had occupied there. God stated, without any possibility of doubt, His displeasure in everything that had gone on in that city. In like manner, He has stated the displeasure and absolute

Separation from the World

hatred that He has for every humanmade system upon this earth. Every single aspect of humanity and their humanmade systems is in opposition to Him, and His plans for them. Everything in this world stands in enmity to His Son.

Right from the beginning of recorded history, we have the hatred God had for the governments and civilizations of humanity. It is in the account of the Tower of Babel. The building of this structure indicated the antagonism that the citizens of Shinar held towards the Lord.

Their attitude was in their statement regarding their relationship with God.

> "Go to, let us build us a city and a tower, whose top
> may reach unto Heaven" Gen. 11:4).

The land of Shinar, and the tower, Babel, built there, came directly under the judging hand of God. In building both the city and the tower, they showed their hatred of God. History tells us that the tower was constructed to worship the sun, moon, and heavenly bodies. Countries have worshiped the sun and moon right from the inception of history. Major civilizations and societies were established on the worship of the heavenly bodies. Sacrifices were made to them. Much blood was shed, and many moral sins were committed in the worship of these gods. The sins and injustices done in the names of these celestial bodies are immense. That these city-states, were identified with idol worship is undeniable. It was combined with the service and worship of the Devil and his hosts. It was an act of rebellion against God. They were stating that they no longer needed God in their lives. They were now free to live their lives independently of any recognition of God or His will for them. They were no longer accountable to anyone other than themselves, and those whom they gave their allegiance willingly. That is all seen in idol worship, along with many other types of rebellion against God. The wickedness and godless activities associated with the worship of idols is well documented. That shows to us the hatred humanity and their political systems have for God.

51

Joseph John Bowman

If the condition were such at the beginning, "have things got any better as time has passed?" "Does a more complex civilization and greater intellectual gains make us morally superior? Have we found a way to stop the wars and international conflicts that are ongoing around the world? Do we have a handle on the economic malaise that has paralyzed our financial systems? Have our moral and ethical standards gotten any better despite our advancements in all the realms of knowledge and science? We have put men on the moon and sent spacecraft to the farthest reaches of our solar system. "Has any of that made us more acceptable before God?"

If they have not, "should we identify ourselves with a system that is under the judgment of God?"

(The father of the kingdom, which Babel became, was Nimrod. He was a son of Ham whose descendants were under the curse of Noah in Genesis 10:8-10.

Nimrod was called a mighty hunter before the Lord.

> "And Cush begat Nimrod: he began to be a mighty one in the earth. He was a mighty hunter before the Lord: wherefore it is said, even as Nimrod the mighty hunter before the Lord. And the beginning of his kingdom was Babel, and Erech, and Accad, and Calneh, in the land of Shinar" (Gen. 10:8-10).

The word for mighty is better read that he was a warrior or tyrant going out from before the Lord. Saying that he was going out from before the Lord is in no way implying that he was under the blessing or sanction of God.

Instead, it is stating that he lived a life of rebellion against God of Heaven.

> "Nimrod was a tyrant from before the Lord" (Gen 10:9).

52

Separation from the World

The people of God looked back on their genealogies until Adam. That was how the people of God viewed Nimrod.

> "And Cush begat Nimrod: he began to be mighty (a mighty tyrant or warrior – Ed.) upon the earth" (1 Chron. 1:10).

That is a better description of Nimrod. His life was typified by rebellion and disobedience against the God of Heaven. His reputation from the beginning was that he was a warrior or tyrant on the earth. Even at this early date, Nimrod had a reputation for being a dictator and ruler who governed over his people as an absolute ruler. His reputation has survived throughout history, as the founder of these godless cities and establishing their pagan religions. Looking at him, we see a man whose entire life was in opposition to God, and God's will for humanity.

It was Nimrod who founded Babel and the civilization that accompanied it. The very name of the tower, Babel, is used in conjunction with the thought of the judgment of God. As we think of the governments and civilizations of man, we should be aware that God has promised to bring every evil work of theirs into judgment.

(For a more accurate depiction of this wicked city and what it stood for, read the very well researched book "The Two Babylons" by Alexander Hislop.)

It was Nimrod and his followers who God judged. To judge the world, God went down and confused their languages. The result was that they would spread over the face of the whole earth. God's judgment was because of their wickedness and rebellion against Him.

> "And the Lord said, Behold the people is one, and they have all one language; and this they begin to do: and now nothing will be restrained from them, which they have imagined to do. Go to, let us go down,

Joseph John Bowman

and there confound their language, that they may not understand one another's speech" (Gen. 11:6-8).

All the languages of the earth exist today because of the judgment of God upon the first city and civilization organized upon this earth. If God hated and judged the first city, why should we think that His hatred is any less for the civilizations that followed. Significantly, the effects of this judgment are still in existence today. It keeps countries separate from each other, as well as keeping them distinct in other ways. This is despite all the efforts of man to find a common language by which means he can communicate. While this works in some ways, it does not work in others. There will never be a unified language upon this earth until the Kingdom Age comes, and God lifts His curse from this earth. It will be when Christ reigns supreme.

Until that day, the plan of God was for humanity to cover the face of the earth. It was never God's desire that men congregate in large metropolitan areas. He wanted us to live in dependence on Him.

God told Adam after he had sinned,

> "Cursed is the ground for thy sake: in sorrow shalt thou eat of it all the days of thy life: thorns also and thistles shall it bring forth to thee: and thou shalt eat the herb of the field: in the sweat of thy face shalt thou eat bread, till thou return unto the ground: for out of it wast thou taken: for dust thou art, and unto dust shalt thou return" (Gen. 3:17-19).

Instead of obeying the command and desires of God, men built large cities. They then formed political systems to rule them. They no longer looked to the Lord of Heaven and earth as their Ruler. They sought their ways, and as a result, they came under the judging hand of God.

After the flood, God gave humanity another opportunity to start over again. His will for them was that they bear children and fill the earth

Separation from the World

with their offspring. His plan was for them to live before Him and acknowledge Him as their King and Lord of all.

He told Noah,

> "Be ye fruitful and multiply; bring forth abundantly in the earth, and multiply therein." (Gen. 9:7).

It was God's divine plan that humanity spread throughout the face of the whole earth, not that they remain settled in some major centers. It was against the mind and plan of God. God called Abraham out of all it identified. In like manner, the cities today resemble Ur which was a major center of idol worship.

Looking at the wickedness of this worlds civilizations we have the picture or Pergamos.

God viewed Pergamos as the,

> "Place where Satan's seat was" (Rev. 2:13).

The word seat can be better read as a throne. It was where Satan ruled. Pergamos, and in like manner Ur, and all other of these godless civilizations were where Satan dwelt. His throne was set up in that city. It was the center of his rule and from which his power emanated. He ruled there in all his power. His wickedness and rebellion against the God of Heaven were evident in all the activities he inspired. His hand is in all the hatred and violence in these centers where man rules. There is nothing about them that shows the love and grace of God. God's mercy and desire for humanity to return to Him were absent. All that was found among these cities were humanities hatred of God. They rebelled against all that God stands for, either now or in eternity. Humanity lost any desire to be accountable to anyone other than themselves. It is all found in the fact that Satan ruled supreme in that place. As a result, the place came under the curse of God.

Joseph John Bowman

As Satan dwelt in Pergamos, so he dwelt in Ur. Likewise, he and his hosts dwell in every center of civilization on this earth. God's was calling Abraham from a center of Devil worship to serve the living and true God. By Abraham's calling from the city-state, we have his departure from the principal place of the civilization of the day. He was rejecting the administrative positions and stands that would have been available to him if he stayed. Both of these are and were, against the will and plan of God for His people.

In Scripture, a city is a place of godlessness, violence, and immorality along with the idolatry that accompanies it.

There is nothing that honors God in the confusion and wickedness of city life.

> "But the wicked are like the troubled sea, when it cannot rest, whose waters cast up mire and dirt. There is no peace saith, my God, to the wicked" (Is. 57:20-21).

God sees the nations of the earth in this way.

> "Woe to the multitude of many people, which make a noise like the noise of the seas; and to the rushing like the rushing of mighty waters: The nations shall rush like the rushing of many waters: but God shall rebuke them, and they shall flee far off, and shall be chased as the chaff of the mountains before the wind, and like a rolling thing before a whirlwind" (Is. 17:12-13).

Reread these verses, and see if there is anything in them that pleases God. If not, then try to explain to a holy God, what justification there is to identify with those who are described.

That is what Abraham was under commandment to leave. We are likewise to leave all that this world speaks of behind us. As we look at this world in all its gross sin and immorality, how hard should it be

Separation from the World

to leave it all behind? However, practically speaking, we are so much like the nation of Israel in the wilderness longing for the cucumbers and melons and leeks and onions and garlic of Egypt (Num. 11:5).

> They longed for all that seemed so pleasant in the past, forgetting the slavery which they had endured. They forgot the whips and mortar and the taskmasters and the bondage they had labored under (Deut. 8:14).

How like them we are!

2. Social Separation

The second area was Abraham's separation from his kinsfolk. It tells of social separation. Then as now, family units were social groupings. It was a much closer degree of separation than the previous one and would have been much more challenging. It was to bid a final goodbye to all his family ties. It included all that was entailed in that relationship. Even today, family groupings and family affairs are significant to the members involved. Those who do not have close relationships, or who have separated from their families feel displaced. They experience a loss of something fundamental. That is what Abraham was asked to leave behind. All the close family relationships that he had built up over the years were to be left behind. The social requirements and engagements that accompany these functions were now things of the past. (They would have been many for Abraham was a very wealthy man.)

The Lord Jesus taught;

> "He that loveth his father or mother more than Me is not worthy of Me: and he that loveth son and daughter more than Me is not worthy of Me" (Matt. 10:37).

Joseph John Bowman

The teaching is that God and the things of God are to come first. He refuses to take second place to anyone or anything.

> "If He is not Lord of all He is not Lord at all."

No relationship, no matter how close physically or emotionally, can ever take a place of precedence over that which our Lord demands. Abraham was asked to leave it all and, by so doing, he was clearly stating that he put God in the first place.

The question we need to answer,

> "Is there anything that we are willing to put in a place of prominence over God?"

That includes every relationship, either personal or professional; or religious or political; as all are important to some individuals. Every affiliation we could ever be involved with needs to be kept in its' proper place of standing.

By so doing, we must exclude some associations, because of the way God views them. It also includes their involvements. In 2 Corinthians 6, God is very definite on the subject of the unequal yoke. Keep this in mind. We will consider the areas we are forbidden by God to spend our time and energy on when we look at that chapter.

Our separation is to be from all who number among the unsaved. It matters not whether they are good and kind or wicked and godless. There are those in our families who hate God. Anything about Him and His people will bring forth expressions of hatred and contempt.

The words of our Lord show the attitudes of the godless towards His people.

> "Now the brother shall betray the brother to death, and the father the son: and children shall rise up against their parents, and shall cause them to be put to death.

And ye shall be hated of all men for My name's sake:"
(Mark 13:12-13).

God called Abraham from association with both the good and kind
as well as those whose lives were in direct rebellion to Him. We
cannot be in partnership or fellowship with the world and still love
and obey Him.

The apostle John exhorts:

> "Love not the world, neither the things that are in the
> world. If any man love the world, the love of the Father
> is not in him. For all that is in the world, the lust of the
> flesh, and the lust of the eyes, and the pride of life is
> not of the Father but is of the world" (1 John 2:15-16).

Separation is to be from every aspect of this world. Every part of
it is sinful and aligned against God. There is nothing about it that
pleases God. Separation is not only from the world in general, it is
from its social activities where primary relationships develop. We
make friendships among them. What will become partnerships often
start as social relationships! More business relationships flourish
on golf courses than anywhere else. Many business unions begin,
and contracts are signed in clubs and resorts. Meetings are made
and concluded in bars and lounges. The leisure lives of many of
the worlds greatest minds are inextricably tied with their financial
interests. Let us be careful not to fall into that web of social activities
and relationships.

Many form social relationships. Many of the business ties formed
result from introductions made at times like these. Relationships
develop as a result of friendships and associations. Marriages
are sometimes formed because of convenience and the joining of
businesses and financial interests. In the end, these friendships are
complicated. Any separation can be painful and may require legal
action. Let us not be ensnared by them. It will make our Christian
life and all associated with it much more complicated. If we take a

Joseph John Bowman

stand for God before the unsaved immediately, they will expect it. It will not be such a battle to leave relationships established earlier.

I recently heard a believer say how meaningful our relationship is with God. In every decision and plan in life, we need to pray to our Father for guidance and direction. We need to keep the following statement in mind. Some of the decisions and relationships we may enter into will not quickly dissolve. Even if we desire, there may be severe impediments to the dissolution of a relationship so entered.

Please keep this little saying in mind as we make decisions about life's directions.

> "If we do not pray about our choices before we make them, we may pray with tears about them later. However, it may be too late for the situation to change as we may have set our life course. As a result of our choices, there may have been a detrimental effect on other believers as well."

As the hymn writer, Joseph Scriven, said when he wrote, "Take it to the Lord in Prayer."

The following hymn writer gives a word of exhortation as we consider how our Saviour desires us to walk. In all things and all ways, His desire and plan are that we be separate from the world, and all of its systems. Ultimately, the word Holy means to be Separate.

Holy, Happy Separation

Holy, happy separation!
They alone are truly blest.
Who from all besides retiring,
And Himself alone desiring
Find in Jesus only rest,
Find in Jesus only rest.

Separation from the World

Jesus calls to separation,
And Himself hath led the way.
His own life the explanation,
His own life the illustration
Who is ready to obey?
Who is ready to obey?

Blessed Jesus, make us willing,
Thus without the camp to go
Unto Thee in glad subjection,
Unto Thee in Thy rejection,
Unto Thee from all below,
Unto Thee from all below.

Separate from all that grieves Thee,
Separate from sinners too;
Yet, like Thee, for sinners caring,
And like Thee, with sinners bearing,
Asking, "What would Jesus do?"
Asking, "What would Jesus do?"

Unto Thee Beloved Master,
Nearer, nearer let us be
Unto Thee in consecration,
Unto Thee in separation,
Ever, only unto Thee,
Ever, only unto Thee!
Lucy Anne Bennett

3. Religious Separation

The last area dealt with was from Abraham's father's house. The teaching is one of religious separation. While this is not directly the subject of this paper, we will cover it, both in this place, as well as under the portion in 2 Corinthinans 6. In many Christian's minds both areas are tied together. They think that because there is a

Joseph John Bowman

so-called Christian party now in existence, or Christians are running for office, we should vote for them. The feeling is that they will have beliefs and take stands we hold. We will, therefore, be able to work in conjunction with them. As they represent us in government, they will work to see that our stands are brought before the government of the day. They are expected to labor in every way possible to seek to have our beliefs made part of the laws of the land. There are certain fallacies to this argument as we will see.

In this section, we will look at Abraham, leaving a world identified with a pagan religion.

We have already mentioned that leaving his father's house speaks of religious separation. In those lands and culture, the head of the house was the family priest. It brings before us the worship of false gods and all it involves. We recognize without any doubt the degree of godlessness that developed from this practice. We should have no hesitation is separating from this aspect of rebellion. God called Abraham out of it, and so it is with us. The religions of this world are not to influence us.

God warned His people of this danger before they entered into the land of Canaan.

> "Take heed to thyself that thou be not snared by following them, after that they be destroyed from before thee; and that thou enquire not after their gods saying, 'How did these nations serve their gods? Even so, will I do likewise.' Thou shalt not do so unto the Lord thy God, for every abomination to the Lord, which He hateth have they done unto their gods" (Deut. 12:30-31).

As God said about the nations of the land in that day, so He is saying of the religions of the world today. It matters not if they are the so-called Christian religions; some have teachings and doctrines that oppose the Bible. Most of these, even though they take on the formal name of

Separation from the World

Christian, deny the God of the Bible, and the truth of the Bible itself. They state that Jesus is "just" a man, albeit a good man, and deny His deity. They say that salvation is to be gained by good works, not faith in Christ. Indeed there is nothing Christian about these religions. Alternatively, we could go on and name all the religions that have come out of the East and the many New-Age religions. (They say a new religion comes out of California every day.) These religions depend, not upon the work of the Cross for salvation. It is the works of men, or even upon that which is demonic that they look for their ultimate salvation. Many depend on the leading of a charismatic leader to tell them how they are to live. Many people put more emphasis on the teachings of some man or woman than on the inspired Word of God. Stay as far away from them as possible. Do not even inquire into them. Even by so doing, we may become contaminated by their evil doctrines. God in His wisdom has told us to keep separate from that which is evil and to cling to that which is good.

May we do so for His name's sake!

The next section, which, in the will of the Lord I plan on covering in some detail, is critical to us today. It deals with that which can relate to the life of every believer.

There is a story that the author, of the following hymn Sir John Bowering, was inspired to write his hymn by a visit to the ruined cathedral on Macao Island near Hong Kong. On top of it stood a blackened cross.

As he viewed what appeared to be a cross in defeat and ruin, he wrote the following words,

Joseph John Bowman

In the Cross of Christ I Glory

In the cross of Christ I glory,
Towering o'er the wrecks of time;
All the light of sacred story
Gathers round its head sublime.

When the woes of life o'ertake me,
Hopes deceive, and fears annoy,
Never shall the cross forsake me,
Lo! It glows with peace and joy.

When the sun of bliss is beaming
Light and love upon my way,
From the cross the radiance streaming
Adds more luster to the day.

Bane and blessing, pain and pleasure,
By the cross are sanctified;
Peace is there that knows no measure,
Joys that through all time abide.

In the cross of Christ I glory,
Towering o'er the wrecks of time;
All the light of sacred story
Gathers round its head sublime.
John Bowering

CHAPTER FOUR –
SEPARATION IN 2 COR. 6

2 Corinthians 6:14-18 is one of the most enlightening passages in the Epistles dealing with separation. In it, is, without doubt, the desire of God for His people. Anyone who reads these verses should not doubt that God wants His people to live lives of separation from the world. It is a clarion call to separation. Like a trumpet sounding over a battlefield, God is declaring His wish in these verses.

God, in the Old Testament, desired the Nation of Israel to be separate from the nations round about them. That being the case, "How does this apply today?" The question is asked, "Do we have the same demands and expectations on us today?" or "Are we under a more liberal dispensation?" "Can we expect to intermingle freely with the world in all its' doings and still experience the blessings of God in our lives?" "Does God have any practical desires to see us living separated lives unto Himself?" Alternatively, "Are we to be indistinguishable from the world in our walk down here?" "What is His desire for the believers walk today?" "Does He make His will understandable, or does He leave the decision up to our conscience?" Is it up to our personal feelings and impressions of the time? Alternatively, "Do we have teachings and tenets easy to understand?" "Is it an impossible doctrine to follow?" Alternatively, "Is it something stated in a manner that even the simplest among us can grasp?" "Is it taught in a way whereby even the youngest believer can take its teachings as their own?" "If the answer to these questions is uncertain or unclear, how can the average believer apply the truths to their daily lives?"

Joseph John Bowman

Most importantly, "What does the Word of God have to say about the subject of separation?" More to the point, "What does God have to say about our separation regarding the politics of this world?"

Let us open the Bible to see what God has to say on this most critical subject.

1. Separation of the Believer in 2 Corinthians 6

In the passage mentioned above, five areas of separation come before the attention of the Church. They cover every region or subject that a believer can experience in their separation from the world. We will not go into all of them extensively. However, they will all come under our consideration. As a result, there will be sufficient to look into at every believers leisure.

First, Paul gave the following verses,

> "Be ye not unequally yoked together with unbelievers; for what fellowship hath righteousness with unrighteousness? And what communion hath light with darkness? And what concord hath Christ with Belial? Or what part hath he that believeth with an infidel? And what agreement hath the temple of God with idols?" (2 Cor. 6:14-16).

Looking at this passage; we will seek to see the meaning. It will be in as transparent a manner as possible and without seeking to complicate the text. However, it is imperative for our understanding to get the meaning of the words in context. It is necessary to take this step to understand these verses.

The exhortation is to

> "Study to show thyself approved unto God, a workman that needeth not to be ashamed, rightly dividing the Word of Truth" (2 Tim. 2:15).

66

Separation from the World

We are entreated to study or be diligent in the effort to get to know and understand the Scriptures. In that way, we must be earnest and trustworthy students of the Word of God. One day, each one should desire to be able to stand before Him and not be ashamed. It all starts with the initial effort of studying God's Word. There are many excellent and dependable study guides available if we look for them. If in doubt, ask those we have confidence in to help as guides and teachers.

I will briefly go over the five points, and then zero in on those I feel will be particularly apt in the study today.

Looking at these various topics; it is evident that God wrote in different ways for a reason. Scripture repeated in different ways is not just to take up space. It is to bring to the attention of the Church different aspects of the truth under consideration.

Before beginning, I want to emphasize that the yoking or fellowship in the passage is between believers and unbelievers. The subject of two believers working together, who, are unsuited spiritually is in other places.

That is not the case here. There can be no misunderstanding or possible misinterpretation of these verses. If there are any problems, it is solely and only because there has been disobedience to the revealed Word of God. The subject covered, deals with a child of God and a child of the evil one seeking to work together in harness. It is an unequal, incompatible partnership.

The yoke always pictures the pulling or working together in unison. I ask the question, "How can we work in unison with someone who is opposed to everything we stand for and believe?" If that is the case, both will be pulling in opposite directions. If we are pulling in harmony with the world, the result is of moving in direct disobedience to God.

Beware for whom we are pulling!

Joseph John Bowman

The picture in this yoking is of an ox with another animal who is unsuited to pull to labor in unision with the oxen. The oxen, being a larger animal, will bear all the weight of the yoke. Any other animal was not capable of pulling harnessed with the oxen.

Thinking about a yoke, our Lord said,

> "For my yoke is easy and my burden is light" (Matt. 11:30).

Being yoked to the unsaved is never easy, and the burden is never light. Why should we place an extra burden upon ourselves more than we already bear? It is inconceivable we would do so voluntarily. Many do so to their detriment, hoping for a peaceful resolution to this union.

For this to take place peacefully, it will take significant concessions by either one side or the other.

> "Are we willing to concede truths that we know are Godly for the sake of peace?"

Alternatively,

> "Will we compromise truths to have a similitude of peace with the ungodly?"

Doing so, "How will we expect the blessing of God?" "How can we compromise Scriptural truths and claim to continue in obedience to Him who has called us out of darkness into His marvelous light?" (1 Peter 2:9)

At the close of this section,

> "Why do we so often put ourselves in a place where our relationship with the world has a greater value than our relationship with Christ?"

CHAPTER FIVE –
THE FIVE SUBJECTS IN
2 CORINTHIANS 6:14-16

1. A Commercial Union Condemned

In 2 Corinthians 6:14-16, Paul shows us five different areas of separation that God desires His people to keep. Separation from the world is in each of these different spheres. We have no freedom to disregard our responsibilities to be separate in any of them. The desire of God for each of us is understandable in this portion.

God in His Word states,

> "Be ye not unequally yoked together with unbelievers: for what fellowship hath righteousness with unrighteousness? And what communion hath light with darkness? And what concord hath Christ with Belial? Or what part hath he that believeth with an infidel? And what agreement hath the temple of God with idols" (2 Cor. 6:14-16).

The Apostle Paul asks;

> "What fellowship hath righteousness with unrighteousness?" (2 Cor. 6:14).

In this question, an economic union with the world comes under the condemnation of God. Let us look at what these words mean. Fellowship means to be "A sharer, an associate." We are not to enter into

69

Joseph John Bowman

a partnership with those who are unrighteous. The unsaved are in this passage. It includes every unsaved soul, no matter how admirable they may be. The unsaved, as God sees them, are corrupt. How can we desire to be in partnership with them? The word unrighteous tells of one who is corrupt, crooked, and immoral. That is how God sees every sinner.

He spoke of their condition in the following words,

> "There is none righteous, no, not one: there is none that understandeth, there is none that seeketh after God" (Rom. 3:10-11).

(These verses are from Psalms 14 & 53. These Psalms, are the words of Almighty God as He views humanity. He declared that none were good among them.)

The Word of God spoke in condemnation on this earth before the flood when He said,

> "The earth was also corrupt before God, and the earth was filled with violence. And God looked upon the earth, and behold, it was corrupt; for all flesh had corrupted his way upon the earth" (Gen. 6:11-12).

Paul continues through the next six verses in Romans 3 describing the unsaved. He came to a conclusion when he said,

> "All have sinned, and come short of the glory of God" (Rom. 3:23).

Are these those with whom we want to identify? Do we want to be numbered amongst them in our business dealings?

Thinking of an associate, the first thought that comes to mind is of a business relationship. There are to be no partnerships or business or commercial ties between one saved by the blood of the Lamb, and an unsaved partner. God condemns every type of partnership or

Separation from the World

relationship of this kind. It includes family if they are unsaved. It may very well mean that we will break a peaceful co-existence. Family unity will never be an excuse to disobey the Word of God.

The Lord Jesus said that He came to bring not peace but a sword on this earth.

> "Think not that I am come to send peace on earth: I came not to send peace, but a sword. For I am come to set a man at variance against his father, and the daughter against her mother, and the daughter-in-law against her mother-in-law. And a man's foes shall be they of his own household" (Matt. 10:34-36).

Partnerships with government agencies need to be looked at carefully. They may mean that the believer will have to compromise his beliefs to keep the peace between them.

(Look at the demands of government for gender equality and acknowledgment. There was recently a headline in the Toronto Sun. It went this way, "Life is befuddling enough without 31 genders." It cited a piece on what has been called gender unbending by a University of Toronto professor Antonella Artuso. In it, he identified 31 separate genders now recognized in the city of New York. As well there are other relationships and acknowledgments that the government demands. We may be able to steer clear of some of these if we are not under their controls. Be very sure that when the government enters into the boardroom of a company, the company loses any Godly controls they may have had previously. Please take this warning. We live in evil times. We are now subject to wickedness a previous generation did not face. As well there are temptations to compromise for expediency that our forefathers did not have.)

We should automatically avoid partnerships — any business relationship that brings a believer under an obligation to the unsaved is at fault. If we are under pressure to compromise our beliefs before God to be successful, we are wrong. We need to ensure from the

Joseph John Bowman

start we are not placing our relationship with God, and His people in a secondary position. Even if the unsaved party has a highly ethical stand, the partnership is wrong.

Bear in mind this saying in the world,

> "Two wrongs do not make a right."

If a relationship starts on the wrong grounds, it will seldom go right. It will never bring the blessing of God in our lives if we disobey His will to further our aims. We may feel that by entering into this association, we will be in a better position to serve the Lord. In everything we do and every relationship we enter, these guidelines are established by God. It is our duty to obey Him, who is Lord.

When the early believers were commanded not to speak about their Lord, they responded,

> "Whether it be right in the sight of God to hearken
> unto you more than unto God, judge ye" (Acts 4:19).

The only other choice is to obey the desires of our minds. If we seek to do what we feel is right in opposition to the plan of God, we will fall under the judging hand of God. There is almost nothing that brings more pleasure to the heart of God than obedience.

God always condemns disobedience.

> "For rebellion is as the sin of witchcraft, and
> stubbornness is as iniquity and idolatry" (1 Sam.15:23).

Before Samuel said the above, he spoke of the high estimation God places on obedience to Him and His will.

> "Hath the Lord as great delight in burnt offerings
> and sacrifices, as in obeying the voice of the Lord?

Separation from the World

Behold, to obey is better than sacrifice, and to hearken
than the fat of rams" (1 Sam. 15:22).

Other stands may take some discretion, but a spiritual man or woman
will know when the relationship has become too close. Beware, as
these are very dangerous affiliations to form and are very difficult
to break.

A dangerous area for believers in this area is money. The losing of it
can be a complicated situation to resolve.

Unfortunately, money can be a deciding factor in many of these
relationships.

> "For the love of money is the root of all evil: which
> while some coveted after, they have erred from the
> faith, and pierced themselves through with many
> sorrows" (1 Tim. 6:10).

It is essential to say that money is not the root of all evil; it is the love
of money. The question is, "Will we do "anything" to make money?"
"Will we compromise our beliefs to enrich ourselves?" "Is making
money the driving force in our lives?" "At the end, how much is
enough?" We need to be very careful that our priorities are right.

> There is an account of John D. Rockefeller. During his
> lifetime he was considered the wealthiest man in the
> world. A reporter asked him towards the end of his
> life, "How much money is enough?" His reply was,
> "Just a little bit more."

Unfortunately, many Christians mortgage their spiritual lives for the
gold of this world.

I want to recite the words of Francis Ridley Havergal's hymn,
"Take My Life and let it be." One of the lines goes, "Take my silver
and my gold; Not a mite would I withhold." Four years after she

Joseph John Bowman

wrote this hymn, she gave many of her possessions to the Church Missionary House. She took the words of her hymn personally and acted practically on them. She obeyed the Scriptural teaching in its words. It was not only theological teaching; it became a fact of life for her. Sadly, too much in our lives is solely knowledge-based. Too little is seen exercised in what is called a "Shoe leather Christian." We are exhorted to put into our daily lives what we have learned theologically.

The hymn following tells how we aught to put our theory into practice.

Take My Life and Let it Be

Take my life and let it be
Consecrated, Lord, to Thee
Take my movements and my days,
Let them flow in endless praise.

Take my hands and let them move
At the impulse of Thy love.
Take my feet and let them be
Swift and beautiful for Thee.

Take my voice and let me sing,
Always, only for my King,
Take my lips and let them be
Filled with messages from Thee.

Take my silver and my gold,
Not a mite would I withhold.
Take my intellect and use
Every power as Thou shalt choose.

Take my will and make it Thine,
It shall be no longer mine.
Take my heart, it is Thine own,
It shall be Thy royal throne.

Separation from the World

Take my love, my Lord I pour
At Thy feet its treasure store.
Take myself and I will be
Ever, only, all for Thee.
Frances Ridley Havergal

2. A Social Union Condemned

The Apostle Paul asks;

"What communion hath light with darkness?" (2 Cor. 6:14).

The word "Communion" means "Social intercourse." Paul made it very clear the type of liaison he was referencing with the word he used.

Paul is not condemning believers meeting together to witness to the unsaved. It is not the condemnation of every kind of legitimate means of spreading the gospel.

The responsibility given to every believer is to,

"Go ye unto all the world, and preach the gospel" (Mark 16:15).

Our duty to those around us is to be a witness to them. Preaching is not only to be public but private. Believers who spread the gospel across Europe and Asia after the death of Stephen were known for their testimonies to the unsaved.

Their reputation was,

"Those who were scattered abroad went everywhere preaching the Word" (Acts 8:4 also Acts 11:19).

Joseph John Bowman

The word preaching is speaking of telling the good news. It is another way of using the word gossiping. The passage is telling us that the believers were spreading the gospel in a personal manner to those with whom they came into contact.

The Apostle Paul said to the elders at Ephesus before he left them,

> "Whereas, I take you to record this day, that I am pure from the blood of all men. For I have not shunned to declare unto you all the counsel of God" (Acts 20:26-27).

What a marvelous thing it would be to be able to say, standing before God, that we have been faithful witnesses for Him. It should be both before the world as well as before the Saints. We are now beyond reproach.

The gospel entrusted to us is summed up by Paul,

> "Moreover, brethren, I declare unto you the gospel which I preached unto you…...For I delivered unto you first of all that which I also received, how that Christ died for our sins according to the Scriptures: and that He was buried, and that He rose again the third day according to the Scriptures" (1 Cor. 15:1 & 3-4).

The message was not to have any limitations put on it. It was to go to all.

The work of our Great High Priest is described by saying;

> "Wherefore He is able also to save them to the uttermost that come unto God by Him, seeing He ever liveth to make intercession for them" (Heb. 7:25).

We sometimes say,

> "He can save from the uttermost to the guttermost."

Separation from the World

How true that is!

We have the exhortation of the Lord,

> "And He said unto them, Go ye into all the world, and
> preach the gospel to every creature" (Mark 16:15).

We are not to limit those to whom we witness. In Acts 11:19, the word for preaching is more commonly used for gossiping. It was to spread from house to house. While some will preach publicly, others will testify privately. We are to speak to those we come in contact with daily. The main thing is that we spread the gospel all around. We all have different areas of influence. You will be able to reach those another believer can have no influence over. The same truth applies to all of us. That is why God has placed every believer in the place where they are. It includes not only where they are geographically, but locally in their places of work and residence. God has a plan for the service and testimony for each of His people. God has placed no limitations over how to spread the gospel. The only regulations on us are that we are to witness to the honor and glory of God.

Our testimony or service is not to be in association with this world or those in it. No believer should be dependent on the unsaved to be able to be a witness. Even the youngest believer can tell you that God will find no pleasure or acceptability in the service of those who are His enemies.

The Apostle John gave a word of commendation to those who were under no obligation to the unsaved in their service to God.

He said, speaking of the Gentiles as the unsaved,

> "Because that for His name's sake, they went forth
> taking nothing of the Gentiles" (3 John 1:7)

Since the unsaved occupy this position, how can we take them into a place of closeness? How can we even imagine, in our wildest

Joseph John Bowman

moments that a union of this sort will bring pleasure to the heart of God?

We have the Word of God saying,

> "Can two walk together, except they be agreed?"
> (Amos 3:3).

In our Bible, walking together always indicates those involved being in fellowship with each other. The question was, "Can two individuals who are not in fellowship on their most fundamental beliefs walk in fellowship together?" Can we be in fellowship with those who hate the One who is most dear to us? Can our closest acquaintances be those who hate our Lord and despise His teachings and commandments for them?

We need to be careful not to get caught into the web of the social structure of this world. We need to beware of getting caught into the trap of this worlds friendships and activities.

Paul was describing the work of the people of God as warfare. He said that our service to Him was the same as a soldier on the battlefield. In everything, we do, we are to realize that we are soldiers in God's army. The word used for a soldier is of a common soldier, one who has no rank. We are under the command of God and cannot command or direct.

In the life of a believer:

> "No man that warreth entangleth himself with the affairs of this life; that he may please Him who hath chosen him to be a soldier" (2 Tim. 2:4).

The following question was asked by Ajai Prakash,

> "Is your Church a Cruise-Ship or a Battleship?"

Separation from the World

Each of us needs to ask the same question honestly of ourselves as we look at our service for God.

The word entangle means to knit into or entwined into its form. We are not to become part of the fabric of this world. We are to be separate from it in every manner.

Social communion can apply to our joining things like social clubs or getting involved in neighborhood social activities, which although pleasurable have nothing God-honoring about them. These are active ties, that can and will, promote the person and leave God out. Some are only for our popularity in society. They can later lead to getting involved politically. It can result in getting recognized socially. Some prize social acceptance very highly. They desire that what they have attained be passed to their children. Their acknowledgments are to be recognized in the attaiments of their heirs. There can be financial as well as business and political boosts. Some aspirations are recognized as far as achievements in this world. We may gain a name in both our local circles as well as far abroad. It may extend nationally, and as well as including international acclaim.

What will the cost be to the spiritual life of the believer? The very mention of God in these gatherings will cause a faithful believer to be immediately ostracised. Any attempt to speak about Godliness or righteous living will be reviled. Morals and justice will be accosted and put to one side. Ethical actions are now almost nonexistent. There is nothing about these gatherings that is pleasing to God. How could these associations be pleasing to a child of God? One who is a son of the Highest and an heir of God and joint-heir with Jesus Christ should be separate from them. How can we continue in association with those who will revile His holy name? Many enter into these associations with good intentions, but the fear of man keeps them silent, and in the end, they lose any testimonies that they may have had.

Joseph John Bowman

The union condemned in this verse is described as communion between light and darkness. The word implies social intercourse. That sort of union is unfathomable.

On the first day of creation, the action of God is,

> "God divided the light from the darkness" (Gen. 1:4).

Right from the beginning, there was a division between these two entities. It would continue throughout the ages.

A picture of the eternal effects of this truth is in the words of the Lord Jesus.

> "And this is the condemnation, that light is come into the world, and men loved darkness rather than light, because their deeds were evil" (John 3:19).

He is the One who came from God.

> "In Him was life: and the life was the light of men. And the light shineth in darkness: and the darkness comprehended it not". (John 1:4-5).

The Psalmist said,

> "Unto the upright there ariseth <u>Light in the darkness:</u> <u>Who</u> is gracious, and full of compassion, and righteous" (Ps. 112:4).

Isaiah was speaking of the wickedness of this world and the grace of God towards them in the following verse:

> "The people that walked in darkness have seen a Great Light: they that dwell in the land of the shadow of death, upon them hath the Light shined" (Is. 9:2).

Separation from the World

The world that lives in darkness is now offered light from above. Opportunity is given to them to accept it or reject it. What will they do?

The desire of the Lord is,

> "I am come a Light unto the world, that whosoever believeth on Me should not abide in darkness" (John 12:46).

Believers are in this world to witness for Him, and to serve Him to the end, that the lost may experience God's salvation.

Paul said that God sent Him, God's Well-Beloved Son, to

> "Open their eyes, and to turn them from darkness to Light, and from the power of Satan unto God, that they may receive forgiveness of sins, and inheritance among them which are sanctified by faith" (Acts 26:18).

The test believers have is how to witness to the world without becoming like them. We are to be separate from this world and all in it. However, we are to witness to those around. We need to live and work among the unsaved. The danger we face is that we become like them with whom we associate.

There is a saying to believers we would do well to heed,

> "We are to be separate from this world without becoming isolationists."

We are in this world, but we are not to become part of it or its systems.

Paul gave guidelines as we seek to follow and serve Him.

> "No man that warreth entangleth himself with the affairs of this life; that he may please Him who hath chosen him to be a soldier" (2 Tim. 2:4).

Joseph John Bowman

The word entangleth means to knit into or become part of it. Believers are to be separate from this world. Even the world recognizes that we become like those with whom we associate. It is a truth seen in every part of society. Those whose friends are lawless are apt to become like them.

I want to give a few lines from a poem by Colin Powell. He is not speaking about Christianity or the mixture of a believer and unbeliever. However, he is dealing with the same truth.

The fact of it is inescapable.

> "If you run with wolves, you will learn how to howl,
> If you associate with eagles,
> You learn how to soar to great heights.
> A mirror reflects a man's face,
> But what he is really like is shown by the kind of friends he
> chooses.

The simple, but true fact of life is that you become like those with whom you closely associate – for good and the bad.

He closes by saying.

> In Prosperity, Our Friends know Us,
> In Adversity, We Know Our Friends.
> Excellence is not an exception; it is a prevailing attitude."
> Colin Powell

Colin Powell knew both intellectually, as well as experimentally the meanings behind his words. He was an American statesman and a retired four-star general. He served with distinction in the United States Army. He was awarded many honors and medals for his service and was respected both for his service in the forces, as well as his work later.

He said as he looked at his training in the Officer Training Corps.

> "I not only liked it, but I was pretty good at it. That is
> what you really have to look for in life, something that
> you like, and something that you think you are pretty
> good at. And if you can put these two things together,
> then you are on the right track, and just drive on."

I was counseled by my father when young, to make friends and companions with those who were more spiritual. That way, they would be an influence for God on all of my actions. Those that are otherwise will seek to negatively influence my life in regards to the things of the Lord because their interests lie in areas that are in opposition to the things of the Lord.

The writer to the Hebrews gave the believers this word of exhortation,

> "Not forsaking the assembling of yourselves together
> as the manner of some is: but exhorting one another:
> and so much the more as ye see the day approaching"
> (Heb. 10:25).

Many believers seek to walk as close to the line as they can. They want to be friends with the world and acceptable to believers at the same time. The picture is. "How close to the edge of the cliff do we want to walk?" "Do we want to take the chance of falling over?" "Do we want the slightest slip to take us over the edge?" We are exhorted to stay as far from the world and its activities as we can.

We will then be protected by Him who has promised:

> "I will never leave thee, nor forsake thee. So that we
> may boldly say, The Lord is my helper, and I will not
> fear what man shall do unto me" (Heb. 13:5-6).

If we are looking for friendship and help socially, we cannot do worse than the people of God.

Joseph John Bowman

Even if they fail, there is the One who has promised,

> "Come unto Me, all ye that labor and are heavy laden, and I will give you rest. Take My yoke upon you and learn of me; for I am meek and lowly of heart: and ye shall find rest unto your soul. For My yoke is easy, and My burden is light" (Matt. 11:28-30).

3. A Political Union Condemned

The third section deals with political separation.

Paul describes it by saying

> "What concord hath Christ with Belial?" (2 Cor. 6:15).

The point under discussion will compare the two leaders we have a choice to follow. The choices we have entered into every avenue of life there is. Whatever decision we make, we will have to decide whose leadership we will follow.

When the Nation of Israel moved in rebellion to God Moses cried,

> "Who is on the Lord's side? Let him come unto me"
> (Ex. 32:26).

Again we have the words of Joshua as he was about to lead the Nation into the Land of Canaan.

He gave them a choice,

> "Choose ye this day whom ye will serve" (Josh. 24:15).

He went on to describe all of their past areas of worship and future choices.

Separation from the World

He closed by saying,

> "But as for me and my house, we will serve the Lord"
> (Josh. 24:15).

There should be no discussion involved as to whom we will follow.

The writer to the Hebrews describes Him in this manner.

> "Looking unto Jesus the Author and Finisher of our
> faith" (Heb. 12:2).

He is the only One whom we should be looking to for our leadership.

We will go into this subject in more depth later.

4. An Ecclesiastical Union Condemned

The fourth part of 2 Corinthians 6:15 deals with an ecclesiastical separation.

> "What part hath he that believeth with an infidel?"
> (2 Cor. 6:15).

God's desire has always been that His people remain separate from the peoples and religions of the lands around them. There is a great danger to be avoided at all costs by entering into alliances with the world's religions. God's people can, and will, compromise the truth by entering into a partnership in this manner. Failure will be the result; rather than submitting to God about any of the challenges they may face. Any seeming inconveniences they may have to deal with to continue worshipping God in a Scriptural manner will be compromised for the sake of peace. Many Saints, in what were once God-fearing denominations, have compromised every aspect of the truth that they once held dear, and now are left with nothing of substance.

Joseph John Bowman

The above tragedy occurred many times to the people of God in Old Testament days. They entered into various types of interrelationships with the nations. Almost, immediately, the worship of false gods and the erection of altars to the worship of their gods took place. At the same time, there was a break down in every type of Godly separation. Intermarriage with the godless took place. Commercial unions came into being. Their morals became like unto the world. They worshipped the gods of the nations around them. It became a deplorable situation. In it, they grieved God.

The ultimate farce as far as any semblance of God-honoring religions are organizations such as "The World Council of Churches." The eventual goal is the amalgamation of all the denominations and Churches together into a "One World Church." It is what has been called the "Ecumenical Movement." All of the groups of leaders of the various religions are meeting together to discuss their union. These unions envision a universal gathering of all the Christian places of worship. The only way this will be accomplished is through major concessions on truth. The end of this movement is that it brings together not only all Christian Churches, but includes every other group. The end is a worldwide religion envisioned by the New Age Movement. All that is accomplished is to marginalize of anything of God and the majorization of everything associated with man. The Word of God condemns any union or fraternization between the Church of God and the religions of this world; attractive as they might be.

(Just a short note before we go on. Beauty does not automatically imply the presence of God. Look at the religious temples and admire the architectural wonders of this world; we must remember that they, and the religious systems they represent, are without God.)

A believer went through some of the great cathedrals of Europe. He looked at the beautiful architecture, and the magnificent carvings and all the beauty and wealth humanity put together to worship a God they did not know. He saw the solemnity of the services and all the pomp and ceremony of humanity. He listened to the awesome music of the organs and choirs. He saw the officials in their grandiose robes, resplendent in all their august authority. He was awed by their solemn ceremonies and regal appearance. As he heard them, they seemed to sing the very songs of Heaven. He heard the beauties of the choirs as they sang majestic songs. The orchestras that accompanied them were beyond description. The whole of their worship was almost unfathomable.

Sadly, they were gathered together to worship a God who was unknown to them. He is One whom they neither knew nor served. He saw the best that a man could put together to worship a God that they did not know and whom they did not love. The very majesty of the cathedrals where God was to be honored and glorified were commendations and tributes to the men who had built these monumental buildings. The musicians who composed and played the music and songs of worship that they had played are exalted. The canticles and oratorios they sang so beautifully were to the exaltation of those who performed them. Instead of these being places where man honored God, the memories of men were being extolled rather than the God, who had created them.

As he witnessed all we have described and more, the words of Paul on Mars Hill in Athens came to mind.

> "God that made the world and all things therein, seeing that He is Lord of Heaven and earth, dwelleth not in temples made with hands, neither is worshipped with men's hands as though He needed anything" (Acts 17:24-25).

In everything, he saw there was nothing that displayed the humility of man before the greatness of God. It all was a display of how great and powerful man was and showed his abilities and wealth. All the wealth and riches of humanity do not impress God. Their abilities and knowledge are as nothing to Him. We have but to go to Job 38 & 39 to see the power of God compared to the weakness of man. Seek to answer these questions by God. Here are a few of them.

Joseph John Bowman

If any of us feel able, go over all of the questions in both chapters. Man is impressed by what he has accomplished and tries to use them to impress God. Even the most knowledgeable among us need to acknowledge our inability to answer these points. If we cannot deal with the essential points of where we came from and our start from nothing, how can we do anything else to impress the God who created us?

God started by asking:

> "Where wast thou when I laid the foundation of the earth?" (Job 38:4).

If we do not know how we were established God asks,

> "Canst thou bind the sweet influences of Pleiades, or loose the bands of Orion? Canst thou bring forth Mazzaroth in his season? Or canst thou guide Arcturus with his sons? Knowest thou the ordinances of Heaven? Canst thou set the dominion thereof in the earth?" (Job 38:31-33).

The questions go on and on. Instead of marveling and worshipping the works of humanity, we are to worship the God who created all things. We will please Him who paid such a monumental price to save us. Otherwise, we will be honoring humanity whose aim is to discredit our Saviour.

These great religions and mighty edifices are but monuments to the power and wealth and intelligence of man. God and all that honors Him is ignored. We have concentrated our sights on things of the world rather than the things of God. When we look at them; we marvel at man's power and ability and mighty wealth. There is nothing in them that tells us of the grace of God. As a result of all mentioned previously, and much more besides, God is telling everyone of His people to stay as far away from this world's religions as we can.

Separation from the World

He told His people in the Old Testament not even to inquire after them.

> "Take heed to thyself that thou be not snared by following them, after that they be destroyed from before thee and that thou enquire not after their gods saying, "How did these nations serve their gods? Even so, will I do likewise." Thou shalt not do so unto the Lord thy God; for every abomination to the Lord, which He hateth, have they done unto their gods" (Deut. 12:30-31).

By so doing, they could be contaminated just by association. It is also a protection. I have seen this enacted more than once. Believers studied various false groups to be able to witness more effectively. Sadly, they became confused, and have now left the gathering of the Lord's people. Some of them go nowhere, while others even go to the places they were studying. So, please, for the sake of the spiritual life within us, stay clear of all that does not honor and glorify God. Consider the testimony of the local gathering place.

The final word for every believer's life is,

> "Come out from among them and be ye separate saith the Lord and touch not the unclean thing and I will receive you saith the Lord" (2 Cor. 6:17).

5. A Matrimonial Union Condemned

The fifth, and last, area of separation deals with marriage.

The verse reads,

> "And what agreement hath the temple of God with idols for ye are the temple of the living God?" (2 Cor. 6:16).

89

Joseph John Bowman

Matrimony is the area of separation in our lives believers stress most often. It is because of the importance of the decision involved and its far-reaching implications. If a believer marries an unsaved partner, it will not only hurt their spiritual life but of children who may be born into that relationship.

As done previously, let us look at, the words used, and how they relate to us.

The first word we come across is "Agreement," and it means, "A deposition of sentiment, in company with, in accord with." The word used to translate the Greek word is agreement. The word brings before us the personal nature of the agreement. It brings us into the emotional area reserved for a husband and wife. It describes the primary requirement for a successful marriage union.

In this passage; God unequivocally condemns this union because it brings into an intimate relationship one of His people and a child of the Devil.

As we have looked at the meaning of the word, it is essential to note that this is the only time this word is in our New Testament. It emphasizes the importance of this word in context. There is to be no romantic love exchanged between one of the Lord's and a follower of Satan. It includes every unsaved person, no matter who they are and how likable they may be. Even though some may have higher moral standards than we do, any marital relationship is forbidden.

The same truth is brought before us by Amos,

> "Can two walk together except they be agreed?"
> (Amos 3:3).

Walking together always speaks of fellowship. Amos is telling us that unless there is total and absolute agreement, there can be no fellowship between any two parties. The Hebrew word "Be agreed"

Separation from the World

means "To fix upon (by agreement); by implication, to meet (at a stated time) to engage (for marriage)."

No matter which meaning used, for any degree of fellowship to take place takes complete and utter agreement. That kind of agreement could never take place between a Christian and an unbeliever.

Any union between a saved and unsaved partner will have catastrophic effects. Initially, it will cause a loss of fellowship between God and a believer. By entering into this union, a believer has moved in direct disobedience against the will of God. Our fellowship with fellow believers is disrupted. We will not be able to enjoy their fellowship as we once did. Even more seriously, it will affect our children. Instead of being born into a home which honors God, and the gospel is taught, these children will be brought up under the influence of the world. The world and the god of this world, desire that they die in their sins. There is nothing that makes this world happier than seeing a Christian fail in their testimony — following that they seek to destroy any spiritual interest or desire on the part of their unsaved friends. It is almost beyond comprehension that a believer would place their children in this position purposely. We are to be on guard that we do not fall into this sin. Pray God that He would preserve each one of us.

The picture of this union should repel every believer. It is an agreement between God and idols. Our God in all of His holiness and righteous judgment is placed on a par with the wickedness and immorality of idols. The God of the universe is compared to an idol, which is nothing.

The Psalmist dealt with this subject when he said,

> "Wherefore should the heathen say, Where is their God? But our God is in the heavens: He hath done whatsoever He hath pleased. Their idols are silver and gold, the work of men's hands. They have mouths, but they speak not: eyes have they, but they see not: they

Joseph John Bowman

have hands, but they handle not: feet have they, but
they walk not: neither speak they through their throat.
They that make them are like unto them; so is every
one that trusteth in them" (Ps. 115:2-8).

How can we have the temerity to fellowship with one whom God
describes in this manner? God goes on to tell every believer that they
are the temple of God. God lives in us and among us. How can we
defile the holy temple of God by being brought into a relationship that
places Him on an equal par with the idols of this earth? We should be
ashamed of ourselves for even considering such a union.

At the close of this section dealing with the separation of every
believer from the things of this earth, we will leave with a hymn
telling us we should stand proudly in our Savior's name. Let us not
be ashamed to stand for Him. When it comes to bearing witness for
His blest name, let us be firm in our position. Let us not falter in our
beliefs. Looking at all this world has, we must recognize it is but for
a season. We have a greater hope.

Let us bear this word of exhortation.

Ashamed of Jesus

Jesus! And shall it ever be!
A mortal man ashamed of Thee?
Ahamed of Thee, whom angels praise,
Whose glories shine through endless days?

Ashamed of Jesus! Sooner far
Let evening blush to own a star.
He sheds the beams of light divine
O'er this benighted soul of mine.

Separation from the World

Ashamed of Jesus? Just as soon
Let midnight be ashamed of noon.
'Tis midnight with my soul till He,
Bright Morning Star, bids darkness flee.

Ashamed of Jesus! That dear Friend
On whom my hopes of Heaven depend?
No, when I blush, be this my shame,
That I no more revere His name.

Ashamed of Jesus! Yes, I may,
When I've no crimes to wash away;
No tear to wipe, no joy to crave,
No fears to quell, no soul to save.

Till then (nor is my boasting vain),
Till then, I boast Saviour slain:
And, oh, may this my portion be,
That Christ is not ashamed of me!

Joseph Grigg
Altered by
Benjamin Francis

CHAPTER SIX –
POLITICAL SEPARATION

The next chapter starts with,

> "And what concord hath Christ with Belial?"
> (2 Cor. 6:15).

The word "Concord" has the meaning of "Accordance" or "Accord." Its root means "To be harmonious, or agree by contract." These words give us the thought of political accord, for the desire of all politicians is harmony. Every single one of them seeks to accede to the will of the people, and therefore do what they want.

That is how they get into power and how they stay in power.

There is a saying,

> "Do not rock the boat."

That attitude is brought out in all of the decisions of every human government. Mankinds rulers in general, govern by polls, and polls indicate the will of the majority. Their will is what sways the policies of the governments. As politicians see the stands of the populace on various issues, it helps make their stands on these various positions firmer. However, if the position of the populace changes, the stands of their politicians does as well. It is not only sad but deplorable that the primary means of gaining the trust of the people causes them to change their policies. To keep in the good standing of the populace, politicians will have no trouble changing their point of view. It is what is known as a flip-flop.

Separation from the World

Many politicians have a reputation for their uncertain stands on many policies. Many political platforms are promises which politicians have no intention of fulfilling. They know that they will never be able to do what they have promised. Their promises are so far beyond their reach it is ridiculous. Among reasonable people, their statements would be called lies. However, the population of these countries expects nothing more from their representatives. Instead of holding them accountable for their falsehoods, they are excused. Their changes of position are rationalized. In the end, those they represent are no better than the politicians. They are all sinners. They are all marked by sinful lives.

If they repeat their promises enough times, people will believe them. There is a saying that goes that way.

> "You repeat a lie enough times to enough people you will be believed."

It is not because they are told the truth. It is because of the sheer number of times a lie is asserted. Many people are gullible and will believe anything if it is said enough times and with enough force and conviction. It matters not if it is false. Even if it is proved false, it is often believed. The current president of the United Staes, Donald Trump, has a phrase for the lies and distortions of the truth that are circulating. He calls those who say such things as speakers of "Fake News." Any believer should see the fallacy in this stand. If we have to lie and back lies to gain power, we are on the wrong side. It does not matter how right the ends of the person we are backing seems to be.

There is a saying that says,

> "Two wrongs do not make a right."

Even the world acknowledges that;

> "The ends do not justify the means."

Joseph John Bowman

Let us make sure we do not compromise our beliefs to accomplish that which is not in the will of God.

The only means of government that pleases God is called a Theocracy. It is a government headed by God Himself. In it, all decisions are by the will of God and for the betterment of His people. A Theocracy has been His wish for His people from the very beginning.

All other types of government attractive though they may be, are against God. It includes the Monarchy as well as the different types of Communistic and Socialistic, Marxist, and Fascist regimes. There are various types of dictatorships and the rules by the Shahs and Imans and Rajas and religious elites. Examples of them are the Pope of Rome, and the Ayatollahs and Rabbis, et cetera. The various types of temple priests and Brahmins in Hinduism. There are more leaders among the nations of the world than we can imagine. There are also all the Imperial and Capitalistic types of government. Almost, the worst is Democracy, because it is a form of government that is governed by and accedes to the will of the people.

Their will and their voice are always against God. We see this all through history from Bible days to our current times. The will of the majority is always against God. It is always what the majority wants and desires that sway the laws of the countries. If any government goes against their desires, it will soon be replaced with one that accedes to their will.

One of the first times we see a democratic decision by the people is in the Old Testament. The Nation of Israel was rebelling against the rule of the prophet Samuel. God had set him up to govern the people as His representative. The people desired a king to rule over them like all of the other nations. Even though the other peoples were godless, and pagan worshipping idols, the Nation of Israel sought to be like them.

The cry of the people was,

Separation from the World

"Give us a king to judge us like all the nations"
(1 Sam.8:5).

God's response to Samuel was,

> "Hearken (listen to, pay attention to - Ed.) unto the
> voice of the people in all that they say unto thee: for
> they have not rejected thee, but they have rejected Me,
> that I should not reign over them" (1 Sam. 8:7).

Wherever we go, and to whomever, we speak, that is the attitude
of those around us. The unsaved may be willing to submit to God.
unless it goes against their desires. If what God demands causes them
any hardship or trial, they will stop having anything to do with Him.
They will collectively raise their voices against Him.

The Psalmist said,

> "Why do the heathen rage, and the people imagine
> a vain thing? The kings of the earth set themselves,
> and the rulers take counsel together, against the Lord,
> and against His anointed, saying, Let us break their
> bands asunder, and cast away their cords from us"
> (Ps. 2:1-3).

It was brought out at the trial and crucifixion of the Lord Jesus.

The cry of the people was and is:

> "We will not have this man to reign over us"
> (Luke 19:14).

As such, we, should never identify ourselves with them and raise our
voice with theirs. How can we justify standing in unison with those
whose object is to rebel against the One who loved us and died for us?
He who is our Saviour and Mediator should not experience rebellion
by those whom He redeemed. We sometimes say that we are known

Joseph John Bowman

by the company we keep. Never is this more accurate than when a believer seeks fellowship with the world over the Lord's people.

In this verse, we have mentioned "Christ and Belial." Let us look at these two personages and who and what they represent.

Christ – The Sent One

The title of our Lord, and it is a title and not a name, is the Christ. It means the One sent from God. It is His title in the New Testament for His description in the Old Testament. He was called the Messiah. He came from the days of creation past. Before the creation of the world, our salvation was conceived. In the ages past, the Father sent the Son.

His obedience was in eternity before the creation of time and anything that followed.

> "Then said I, 'Lo I come, in the volume of the book it is written of Me, I delight to do Thy will, O My God" (Ps. 40:7).

The blessings of the Jewish nation were,

> "From the foundation of the world" (Matt. 25:34).

When we see the Church, it is;

> "According as He hath chosen us in Him before the foundation of the world" (Eph. 1:4).

The truth that we were chosen before the creation of the world is dear to the heart of every one of us. He came to do the will of God, and to accomplish His plan for our salvation (Ps. 40:7).

He was the One sent from God with a definite purpose in view.

Separation from the World

> "For what the law could not do, in that it was weak through the flesh, God sending His own Son in the likeness of sinful flesh, and for sin, condemned sin in the flesh; that the righteousness (righteous requirements – Ed.) of the law might be fulfilled in us" (Rom. 8:3).

That is the reason He came. In our natural state, we were unable to do anything to save ourselves. We could not keep the law even partially let alone totally.

That is what the verse means when it says,

> "It was weak through the flesh" (Rom. 8:3).

It was only because of the weakness of our flesh that the law was unable to save us. The Law was perfect. It was in the plan of God for us.

Paul said,

> "Wherefore the law was our schoolmaster to bring us unto Christ, that we might be justified by faith" (Gal. 3:24).

Again Paul said as he discussed the Law and our inability to keep it. It was our inability that made the Law a failure.

It was not that weakness was in the Law.

> "Wherefore the law is holy, and the commandment holy, and just, and good" (Rom. 7;12).

However, we have the truth that

> "What the law could not do, in that it was weak through the flesh, God sending His own Son in the likeness of sinful flesh, and for sin, condemned sin in

Joseph John Bowman

the flesh: that the righteousness of the law might be fulfilled in us, who walk not after the flesh, but after the Spirit" (Rom. 8:3-4).

Our Lord was able to say on the cross,

"After this, Jesus knowing that all things were now accomplished, that the Scripture might be fulfilled, saith, I thirst" (John 19:28).

Scriptural fulfillment occurred at that moment. The perfect Law of God was complete.

We can now read,

"There is therefore now no condemnation to them which are in Christ Jesus, who walk not after the flesh, but after the Spirit " (Rom. 8:1).

Stephen said that humanity has

"Received the Law by the disposition of angels (service of angels – Ed.), and have not kept it" (Acts 7:53).

Despite not having kept the Law, we are not condemned, because there is One who kept it in our place. That is why He came into this world. It is why God sent Him. He was ever The Sent One from the Throne of God.

We are born with a sinful nature, we are prone to sin. Sin comes naturally to us. It was impossible that we keep the holy Law of God in its totality, let alone even partially. It is very clear that the Law's failure to save us had absolutely nothing to do with any weakness or lack that was in the Law. The Law in itself was perfect for it set a perfect standard for man to keep. It was the absolute requirement of a holy God for humanity to meet if they was to enter into Heaven. However, because of man's failure, and God's love for us, He sent His

Separation from the World

only begotten Son into this world to save us. He was the only One who had ever pleased God and, kept every single one of His laws; He is the only One who can save us. So, by God sending Him, a way was planned whereby we might be saved.

(Note: it was "In the likeness of sinful flesh" He came. He was never

"Like sinful flesh."

He was never sinful in any way or action. He came in our likeness in that He was truly human, yet He was never like us.)

The writer to the Hebrews tells us,

"For such an High Priest became us, who is holy, harmless, undefiled, separate from sinners, and made higher than the Heaven" (Heb. 7:26).

He was entirely distinct from us yet like unto us in all ways. We cannot begin to fathom it; we must believe it by faith.

"But when the fullness of time was come, God sent forth His Son" (Gal 4:4).

He sent Him at precisely the right time in both the history of this world and in the timetable that God had planned. There was nothing about His coming into this world that was not planned from the vast ages of eternity past. It was all prepared. God Almighty put His stamp of approval upon it. While He Who became the Sin Bearer in our place was on the cross, He satisfied the demands of a Holy God in regards to sin.

It said about Him,

"Jesus knowing that all things were now accomplished, that the Scriptures might be fulfilled" (John 19:28).

101

Joseph John Bowman

After that, we hear His cry of completion. He had achieved a work that would never need to be redone. The value of it would last for the endless ages of eternity.

He would cry in triumph at the end of His work,

> "It is finished" (John 19:30).

That one act shows us the love of God in a way no other action could do. In it was seen a depth of love that could only be enacted because of His obedience to His Father. He voluntarily submitted Himself to His Father's will. By so doing, salvation was provided for those who were enemies to God.

It is beyond our comprehension what was accomplished on the cross.

> "In this was manifested the love of God toward us because that God sent forth His only begotten Son into the world, that we might live through Him" (1 John 4:9).

In this verse, we have the reason He came. It was so that we who were dead spiritually might live unto God and eternally live in the fullness of life through Him.

One further reference is:

> "The Father sent the Son to be the Savior of the world" (1 John 4:4).

He was sent to provide a means of salvation that was to be accessible to every person upon the face of this world. It was to all. It is only accessible for those who believe in it.

The offer is:

> "Unto all and upon them, that believe" (Rom. 3:22).

Separation from the World

Indeed, as His title means; He is the One sent from God to provide salvation for the lost and perishing in this wicked world that is condemned to spend a lost eternity in Hell if they do not repent. In so doing, He showed forth the love of God to the world that was at enmity to Him. When we view His coming into this world, we see the grace and mercy of God shown forth before our wondering gaze. (The grace of God displays itself in His giving us something that we do not deserve while, in His mercy, we are not receiving that which we so rightly deserve.) Both of these attributes of God are brought forth before us in the salvation He has so freely offered to us as a gift from His gracious hand.

Christ – Our Leader

He was the "Sent One" from God. As such, He is God's appointed Leader. He is the One sent by God Whom we are to follow. We will follow Him into the realms of eternity. In that case, we should not hesitate to follow Him in all the different things we experience in this world.

We are to be

> "Looking unto Jesus, the author (Captain or Leader – Ed.) and finisher (Perfector – Ed.) of our faith" (Heb. 12:2).

He is our Captain. He, therefore, is the One who is in charge. He is the One, and the only One, whom we must serve. As we serve Him, our part is laid out below. The life of a believer is not on beds of ease.

A well-known columnist from days gone by wrote a book. It was titled,

> "If Life is a Bowl of Cherries What am I doing in the Pits?" (Erma Bombeck).

Joseph John Bowman

Believers are not to expect the lives of carefree exultation with no trials or sorrows. We are to expect that we will face trial and tribulation throughout our journey.

Paul tells us to

"Endure hardness, as a good soldier of Jesus Christ" (2 Tim. 2:3).

We are soldiers. We are everyday soldiers on duty. We are not officers or soldiers with any rank whatsoever. We do not, as soldiers in today's armies, hold a commission over those among whom we serve. We are but the humblest of privates; we hold the lowest most common rank in His army. We must serve our Heavenly Master.

Here is a verse of Alfred Tennyson's poem. As we read it, we should ask ourselves,

"If a man will serve in this unflinching manner up to his physical death, should we be any less willing to serve the One who died for us?"

The Charge of the Light Brigade

"Forward the Light Brigade!
Was there any man dismay'd?
Not tho' the soldier knew
Someone had blunder'd
Theirs not to make reply,
Theirs not to question why,
Theirs but to do and die.
Into the valley of Death
Rode the six hundred."

Alfred Lord Tennyson

Separation from the World

This very famous poem outlines to us the attitude of the soldiers of today's armies. Let the same attitude be ours in our service for our Captain. While the captains of today's armies will and can make mistakes, we know that our Heavenly Captain will never make a mistake.

He is our Captain in the above verse. We are to know Him in this way as our Captain and Leader. He is the One who entered into death and with all authority emerged at the other side victorious.

We have the assurance that

> "Through death, He might destroy him that had the power of death, that is the Devil; and deliver them who through fear of death were all their lifetimes subject to bondage" (Heb. 2:14-15).

Indeed, He led us right into the very realms of Satan and destroyed him. He is our Master! We are likened to soldier at war. A good soldier obeys his Captain without questioning the orders.

There is a saying in the world that says,

> "Your will is my command."

In like manner, we are to obey Him without question.

He is not only our Captain; He is our Leader. A leader is someone we follow. A good leader has already gone the way before and knows the problems and pitfalls that we will face. He knows the best way through and has a genuine care for those he is leading. As we apply this truth to Him, we can rest assured in the fact that He will never lead us astray, but that He has a real concern for us and only wants what is the best. He wants to lead us out on the other side in a better condition than when we entered under His leadership and into fellowship with Him. The truth of this teaching is in Psalms 22, 23 & 24.

Joseph John Bowman

The points here briefly are the following. They sum up the whole of our Lord's work on earth among His people. They are a portrayal of His death to His coming again for us.

He is the "Good Shepherd" who died for the sheep. (Compare Psalm 22 – John 19) In His death, He displayed the credentials that made Him worthy of our worship and discipleship. One to be worthy of paying the price of our sins had to fulfill two essential aspects of the offering.

First, He must be willing to pay the ultimate sacrifice. Our Lord willingly came into this world. He offered Himself upon the cross to pay the penalty for our sins. His sacrifice was decided before this world came into being. In the past ages, He offered Himself as the only One who was able to pay the price God demanded. The willingness of His sacrifice is found all through the Holy Scriptures. Read John 3:16 for there the Father sent the Son.

Among many other places, we will read the words of the author of the Hebrews,

> "How much more shall the blood of Christ, who through the eternal Spirit offered Himself without spot to God, purge your conscience (speaks of the cleansing of moral deficiencies – Ed.) from dead works to serve the living God? (Heb. 9:14).

He freely offered Himself to do the work. There never was a moment of hesitation. He gave Himself freely for us all.

Paul said,

> "Who gave Himself for our sins, that He might deliver us from this present evil world, according to the will of God and our Father" (Gal. 1:4).

Separation from the World

He must be able to pay the price demanded. He alone was without sin. He was the only One who could stand before a holy God as our Substitute for sin.

He was the only One whom God could accept as the price for our sins.

> "For such an High Priest became us, who is Holy, harmless, undefiled, separate from sinners, and made higher than the heavens" (Heb. 7:26).

Peter told us about Him. Peter was able to view His life for the three and a half years our Lord walked on earth.

Peter could say, recollecting all that he had seen and heard,

> "Who did no sin, neither was guile fold in His mouth" (1 Pet. 2:22).

He was the only One who was able to pay the penalty for our sins. He alone could lay down His life, and a Holy God would accept the value of the sacrifice as suitable to pay the price for sin.

In these ways, the sacrifice given was both willing and able to pay the final sacrifice. The One who was the Lamb of God could pay the ultimate sacrifice for all if we accepted it for ourselves.

If someone lays down their life for another person, they have shown real care and concern for their well-being. He had this concern for us. He showed His love for us in a way no other man could do. Therefore, He is worthy of being our Leader.

He is the "Great Shepherd" who is living for us. (Look at Psalm 23 – Hebrews 13:20) Because He lives, we have a guarantee from God Almighty that we shall live also. That guarantee given is because of His resurrection from the dead. We have the assurance,

Joseph John Bowman

> "But now is Christ risen from the dead, and become
> the firstfruits of them that slept" (1 Cor. 15:20).

Our Lord rose from the dead and is now seated in Heaven at the right hand of God. He is there as our Great High Priest.

He is now ascended and seated in glory.

> "God also hath highly exalted Him, and given Him
> a name which is above every name: that at the name
> of Jesus every knee should bow, of things in Heaven,
> and things in earth, and things under the earth: and
> that every tongue should confess that Jesus Christ is
> Lord, to the glory of God the Father" (Phil. 2:9-11).

He is living and representing us in Heaven in the presence of God as our Great High Priest. As such, He leads us into the throne room of Heaven; into the presence of a Holy God. One day we will live there with Him throughout all the endless ages of eternity. It is all because He is living in Heaven today. As such, we are not following a dead martyr, but a living Saviour and He alone is worthy of our service.

Finally,

> "Therefore, my beloved brethren, be ye steadfast,
> unmovable, always abounding in the work of the
> Lord, forasmuch as ye know that your labor is not in
> vain in the Lord" (1 Cor. 15:58).

As the "Chief Shepherd" He is coming again for us. (Compare Psalm 24 – 1 Peter 5:4) It is the hope that every believer has that one day He is going to split the heavens, and with the sound of a mighty trumpet and the voice of God Almighty He will call us to be at home with Himself (1Thess. 4:13-18). That hope energizes every believer in their service for Him. It is different from any hopes the unsaved have. For with them, hope is dependent upon luck and good fortune. It is always something that they hope to have, but are unsure of getting.

Separation from the World

The Christian's hope is different. It is a belief centered upon a secure and unassailable fact. While our faith may be shaken, the fact that lies behind our faith will never fail. It is the hope we have centered on the return of the Lord. We do not know when He is coming again; we know that His coming is sure because He promised that as sure as He went away, He was going to return.

> "In My Father's House are many mansions: if it were not so, I would have told you. I go to prepare a place for you. And if I go and prepare a place for you, I will come again, and receive you unto Myself;that where I am, there ye may be also. And whither I go ye know, and the way ye know" (John 14:2-4).

Heaven is described in all its glory. It is where we will spend all of the endless ages of eternity. Heaven will be our eternal Home. It is so glorious, and we will be there not only because of its glory but because of the One who will dwell there in our midst.

> "And He showed me a pure river of water of life, clear as crystal, proceeding out of the Throne of God and of the Lamb. In the midst of the street of it, and on either side of the river, was there the tree of life, which bare twelve manner of fruits, and yielded her fruit every month: and the leaves of the tree were for the healing of the nations. And there shall be no more curse: but the Throne of God and the Lamb shall be in it; and His servants shall serve Him: and they shall see His face; and His name shall be in their foreheads. And there shall be no night there; and they need no candle, neither light of the sun; for the Lord God giveth them light: and they shall reign for ever and ever" (Rev. 11:1-5).

How reassuring it is to have hope in the future that will stand throughout all the uncertainties of the world.

Joseph John Bowman

While, we look at these verses, and many more besides, all that is left for us to do is to follow Him. He is our Leader. He is the Leader whom God ordained. As such, we ought to follow Him. Not as a leader from among men who can and often will lead us astray. Every leader, no matter how good they are, will fail. They will disappoint us and lose our confidence. There will always be something about them that causes us concern. He who is God's chosen Leader will never fail us. He will be with us, faithful to the end. We can depend on Him come what may.

The hymn writer well said,

Guide us, O Thou Great Jehovah

Guide us O Thou great Jehovah,
Pilgrims through this barren land:
We are weak, but Thou art mighty;
Hold us by Thy Powerful hand:
Bread of Heaven
Feed us now and evermore.

Open wide the living fountain
Whence the healing waters flow;
Be Thyself our cloudy pillar
All the dreary desert through:
Strong deliv'rer
Be Thou still our strength and shield.

While we tread this vale of sorrow
May we in Thy love abide;
Keep us, O our gracious Saviour!
Cleaving closely to Thy side:
Still relying
On our Father's changeless love.

Separation from the World

Saviour, come! We long to see Thee
Long to dwell with Thee above:
And to know, in full communion,
All the sweetness of Thy love:
Come, Lord Jesus!
Take Thy waiting people Home."

William Williams Pantyceln

I want to end with a quotation from a respected man of God. Billy Graham labored among us the whole of his life. He was a faithful preacher of the gospel. Under his preaching, a large number of individuals accepted Christ as their Saviour. Only eternity will tell the value of the work he did with such faithfulness for many years.

I want to give a quotation of his as we look at the affairs of this life given in the light of eternity.

"My hope does not rest in the affairs of this world. It rests in Christ who is coming again" (Billy Graham).

Belial – Satan's Leader

There is Belial. "What does his name mean?" "Of whom does the picture speak?" "By viewing him what characteristics come to mind?" "Do his name and character tell us of someone with whom we would desire to associate?" "If not, why not?"

The very meaning of his name symbolizes who and what is involved in his work. His name tells us the kind of leader he is and will be. He is one who is "Worthless, reckless and lawless." His name refers to the lowest type of person or individual. The terms "Sons of Belial" or "Daughter of Belial" is used 15 times in the Old Testament. Its use tells us of a person whom others considered utterly useless and not worthy of their regard. The word is only used once in the New Testament (2 Corinthians 6:15). Bousset thinks that the "Man of Sin" of 2 Thessalonians 2:3 is a

Joseph John Bowman

reference to Belial. (Some read this term as the "Man of Lawlessness.") He states that it is a translation of the name Belial.

Fausset says about Belial in his dictionary,

> "As Satan is opposed to God, and the Anti-Christ opposed to Christ, so does Belial stand in opposition to Christ."

It shows every anti-Christian pollution personified.

Gesenius describes the term as follows,

> "It is in the sense of one unbridled, rebellious, of the lowest condition. It is without usefulness, good for nothing."

In the Old Testament, the use of his name always refers to a useless person. However, the one reference (and maybe two) in the New Testament refers to Satan and Satan's influences in the world. It is a complete description of him and the value of his work.

Belial, in this passage, is Satan's chosen leader. He stands in direct opposition to Christ, God's Chosen Leader.

(Belial when we see him and Beelzebub, who are the same individual, (also Abaddon and Apollyon, – see Revelation 9:11) are in Scripture as some of the chief princes of Satan's domain. While God has a kingdom of righteousness, Satan has a kingdom of evil and wickedness of which it would do us well to be more aware.)

There are different domains, or powers and positions, among the angels of Heaven. So there are among the hosts of Satan's angels. Satan (Lucifer) was the chief of the angels of God. (Read Isaiah 14:12-17 & Ezekiel 28:13-15.) Because of this, when he rebelled against God, a large number of angels followed him. (Revelation 12:1-4 seems to show that when Satan fell, he took a third of the angels of

Separation from the World

Heaven with him.) As holy angels, they occupied different domains in Heaven, and they now hold the same authority in their fallen states. Their authority presently is seen in the respect they are shown. Although they fell because of sin, they have not lost the authority of their past positions.

(An example of this is when someone in authority leaves their previous position. One who was, for example, the President of the United States or the Prime Minister of Canada will always be given that title of respect. So will those who have maintained positions of military responsibility. A general is always a general, and a colonel is always the same. We always address them in a manner that shows our respect for their past achievements.)

It is the attitude of Michael the archangel.

> "Yet, Michael the archangel, when contending with the devil he disputed about the body of Moses, durst not bring against him a railing accusation (to condmen or judge – Ed.), but said, The Lord rebuke thee" (Jude 9).

Since Michael, who was one of the chief angels in Heaven, showed his respect to the Devil much more should we show our respect to those who rule over us on earth. When one of those who is the holiest in creation did not treat the Devil with disrespect, we need to act in the same way. The angels of God did not treat Satan with disrespect. In like manner, we should treat the rulers God has placed over us with respect.

Although Satan cannot be everywhere at once, he has emissaries, some more powerful than others, everywhere. When we come to Daniel 10:13 & 20, we are told of some of their activities and influences away from the realm of this earth; through their influence over it. The chief and only aim of every fallen angel is to defeat God and His Holy Angelic Hosts, through their activities in the heavenlies.

We meet the great red dragon in Revelation 12:1-4, who has seven heads and ten horns with seven crowns upon his heads.

113

Joseph John Bowman

He drew a third of the angels of Heaven down with him.

> "And his tail drew the third part of the stars of Heaven
> and did cast them to the earth" (Rev. 12:4).

(There is no doubt that this is Satan himself and not one of his emissaries. Whether this refers to the original angelic fall or a separate one, later on, we do not know for sure.)

It is important to note that although Satan is mighty and knowledgeable, he is not God. (Satan knows that. Although he sought to rebel against God, he never aspired to be higher than Him.)

He said,

> "I will be like the most High" (Is. 14:14).

He aspired to be like God, not more excellent than Him. He is not God, or as God. He is not omniscient. No matter how much Satan knows, he does not know everything. He has a grasp of the Scriptures. However, he is unable to understand the depths of the Word of God. Only those who are believers can understand the things of God. The following Scripture is describing the ability of the unsaved to understand the things of God. The truth is the same to him whom the unsaved follow. Satan is extremely knowledgeable. He knew much in the past and has learned many things in the ages since. He cannot understand the truths of the things of God. He cannot perceive even the most fundamental truths of Scripture. In his mind and plans, he will one day be triumphant. He desires nothing more than to see the people of God defeated. He wants to thwart the plans of God on earth.

Since their leader cannot understand the wills and plans of God, the same thing must be said about his followers. No matter what the subject is, they cannot understand its truths. Many unsaved individuals can enter into intellectual discussions on the Scriptures. They may outwit some believers. However, they do not understand the truths written on its pages, because they do not know the Author.

Separation from the World

As a result,

> "The natural man receiveth not the things of the Spirit of God: for they are foolishness unto him: neither can he know them, because they are spiritually discerned" (1 Cor. 2:14).

Lucifer before his fall was described:

> "Behold, thou art wiser than Daniel; there is no secret they can hide from thee with thy wisdom and thine understanding thou hast gotten thee riches, and hast gotten gold and silver into thy treasures: by thy great wisdom and by thy traffick hast thou increased thy riches, and thine heart is lifted up because of thy riches" (Ez. 28:3-5).

After Lucifers fall God said,

> "Thine heart was lifted up because of thy beauty, thou hast corrupted thy wisdom by reason of thy brightness: I will cast thee to the ground, I will lay thee before kings, that they may behold thee" (Ez. 28:17).

He cannot know everything. However, we are to beware of his knowledge. He is a fast learner. He has had over six thousand years to learn what works. He has a vast store of knowledge to try the people of God as he goes among them. He started with Eve, and his methods have not changed since then. He was successful then, and he is thriving now.

To defeat him we are told,

> "Submit yourselves therefore to God. Resist the devil, and He will flee from you" (James 4:7).

Joseph John Bowman

He is not omnipotent. He cannot be everywhere at once. However, he has a large number of fallen angels with him. He also has a countless number of demonic hosts at his disposal. We should not belittle his desire to defeat the works of God. His wish in the past is the same as today. He has a desire to be as the Most High God (Is. 14:14). His wish is to cause disorder and disgrace to come upon every aspect of God and His people. We are not to allow him to do his evil work in us. If he wins, it is to our disgrace and the dishonor of God. It will bring reproach on God's holy name. We should seek to avoid such an end.

He is not all-powerful even though he has more power than any other of the creation of God.

It was said about him as he existed in the past,

> "Thou art the anointed cherub that covereth; and I have set thee so: thou wast upon the holy mountains of God; thou hast walked up and down in the midst of the stones of fire. Thou wast perfect in all thy ways from the day that thou was created, until iniquity was found in thee" (Ez. 28:14-15).

Saying this, we realize that we have but a small indication in our lives of the powers that he has. One day, during the Great Tribulation, he will be given full reign to do as he wants, and then we will see his abilities and powers in a way that we cannot now. It is essential, that we keep these realizations before us, as we think upon him, and what his desires are for us They are seen in what he can do. One other glaring weakness he has is that he cannot understand Scriptures. Even at that, he will use the Scriptures to cause discouragement and defeat in the lives of believers. We need to understand that his application of God's Word is always faulty and wrong. He cannot apply the Scriptures of Truth properly.

He is described in the following manner by our Lord.

Every one of his followers is in the same category.

Separation from the World

"Ye are of your father, the devil, and the lusts of
your father ye will do. He was a murderer from the
beginning, and abode not in the truth, because there is
no truth in him. When he speaketh a lie, he speaketh of
his own: for he is a liar, and the father of it" (John 8:44).

Knowledge of the Scriptures is given only by the presence of the
Spirit of God. So while he can read it, he does not understand what
it is saying. He does not understand the role the Church plays or its
conclusion. It is all a puzzle and problem for him.

In the very pictures drawn for us of the princes and domains of
Satan, we see his wickedness as well as his vileness brought forth.
Right at the beginning of this section are some questions we need to
consider, "If the leader who we are being introduced to be of such
a character why should we have any inclination to follow him?" "If
the leader is of such a character, why should we think his followers
will be any better?"

There is a saying,

"A man is known by the company he keeps" Aesop.

Another quotation goes,

"Evil communication corrupts good manners"
Benjamin Banneker.

That is true of those in the world. Make sure it is not true of us.

As we have seen, all that is good and righteous is personified in
Christ; all that which is low and vile is in Belial and ultimately in
Satan.

The question then is, "What concord hath Christ with Belial?"

Joseph John Bowman

The only answer that we can come to is that there can be absolutely no semblance of harmony between the One who is

> "Of purer eyes than to behold evil, and canst not look on iniquity" (Hab. 1:13).

The only other option given to us whom we can serve is he who is evil personified.

The question is,

> "Should we form an unequal yoke with such a one, or with those who are fellowshipping with him?"

Which of these two leaders are we going to follow?

I want to give one other example of the wickedness of those who are in this world. The example is about the prince of the power of the air, who is the leader of those in this world.

Paul warned the Philippians about those who would come in among them from the world.

> "For many walk, of whom I have told you often, and now tell you even weeping, that they are the enemies of the cross of Christ: whose end is destruction, whose God is their belly, and whose glory is in their shame, and who mind earthly things" (Phil. 3:18-19).

As Paul looked on those deceivers, he wept. He wept for their lost souls and for the eternal end that awaited them. He also wept as he thought of the damage they could do to the believers in their local gatherings. As they gathered together in simplicity and faithfulness, it would all be destroyed by the incursion of the wicked doctrine of these whom Paul called enemies of the cross of Christ. (Enemies is the same word used for Satan as the Deceiver.) The verse that followed gives us a description of the deceivers. It is also an accurate

Separation from the World

description of him who is the Deceiver of the brethren. He who has the ultimate job of deceiving the people of God is described. The end of the unsaved is Perdition. They will experience destruction ultimately. It will last for all eternity. The pains and sorrows of the lost will never end. The horrors associated with that end are indescribable.

The one the unsaved worships is he who supplies them all their fleshly desires. They glory in all he supplies to them. In days past many of these things were shameful to the world. The world glories in them now. It has even come to the extent where the world persecutes and puts to shame those who do not practice and endorse these corrupt activities. In the end, the whole focus of their minds is on the things of this world. There is nothing of God about them.

God is not in their hearts or their minds.

> "As it is written, there is none righteous, no, not one: there is none that understandeth, there is none that seeketh after God. They are all gone out of the way, they are together become unprofitable: there is none that doeth good, no, not one: their throat is an open sepulcher: with their tongues they have used deceit: the poison of asps is under their lips: whose mouth is full of cursing and bitterness: their feet are swift to shed blood: destruction and misery are in their ways: and the way of peace have they not known: there is no fear of God before their eyes" (Rom. 3:10-18).

When we see those around us described in this manner, how could we justify any partnership with them? In that case, how would we ever have the temerity or brass even temporarily to follow him who their leader? He whom they follow is Belial! The prince of filth and wickedness. He is the one whose chief pursuit is to deceive us. He seeks to destroy the works of God. Why would we have anything to do with him or his kingdom

Joseph John Bowman

At the close of this section, I want to leave with another quotation from our brother Billy Graham. Throughout his service, he had one aim in view. It was to please Him who had called him to His service.

Let us evaluate our service in light of the following words. Bear in mind the differences between the two leaders involved. Look at their purposes for us and their aims for our eternal destinies.

Billy Graham said,

> "God has a plan, and the Devil has a plan, and you
> have to decide which plan you fit into" (Billy Graham).

Choose the glory of God and the one which will result in our receiving crowns and praises from Him who paid a price of such an enormous value to redeem us. Only then will we know that our lives had been worth the costs paid for them.

We will then recognize the value of the words of the writer to the Hebrews,

> "For He hath said, I will never leave thee, nor forsake
> thee. So that we may boldly say, the Lord is my
> Helper, and I will not fear what man can do unto me"
> (Heb. 13:5-6).

I will leave with the words Joshua gave to the Nation of Isreal.

He left them with a choice of leaders and whom they would follow,

> "And if it seem evil unto you to serve the Lord,
> Choose you this day whom ye will serve; whether
> the gods which your fathers served that were on the
> other side of the flood, or the gods of the Amorites in
> whose land ye dwell: But as for me and my house, we
> will serve the Lord" (Josh. 24:15).

Separation from the World

We will follow either the One or the other. The choice is ours to make. Make it wisely.

The Wickedness of Government

We have looked at the two leaders we have a choice to follow. Satan's description was portrayed. His description pictures to us the leaders of this world. Even this world acknowledges that we will become like those with whom we associate. It, in itself, should keep us away from the politics and political systems found here. Our place is in Christ.

We have our citizenship,

> "For our conversation (politics – citizenship – Ed.) is
> in Heaven, from whence also we look for the Savior,
> the Lord Jesus Christ" (Phil 3:20).

Our political allegiance is in Heaven and to be to Him, who is our Great High Priest. Someday He is going to come and lead us into the presence of God. Why then, on earth, should we lend our support to an earthly leader, impressive though he or she maybe? All they can do is to try to change affairs in their little corner of the earth. (They probably will not be able to do much there either.) However, our Lord can bring us directly into the August presence of the God of the universe. He will fulfill that work both now and in eternity. There should be no choice who we should follow!

God has established the leaders of this earth for His purposes, let us leave the choice of who they will be unto God. Many believers give lip service to the previous statement. Despite that, they hold that believers have both a right and a privilege and responsibility to seek to put the right person into power. To do this, we are required to vote for the one whom we feel God would have to rule over the affairs of man. As we think in this way, let us keep before us that it is God who puts individuals into positions of power. He will remove them when their work is done. It is His work. He alone knows when

121

Joseph John Bowman

it will be completed to fulfill the desires of His will. We have no part to play in His government of the universe. Likewise, we are not to involve ourselves in the governmental actions of this world, because He alone is King of kings.

<u>Sound the High Praises of Jesus the King</u>

Sound the high praises of Jesus, the King!
He came and He conquered – His victory sing;
Sing, for the power of the tyrant is broken;
The triumph complete over death and the grave.
Vain is their boasting; Jehovah hath spoken,
And Jesus proclaimed Himself mighty to save.
Sound the high praises of Jesus the King!
He came and He conquered – His victory sing.

Praise to the Conqueror! Praise to the Lord!
The enemy quailed at the might of His word;
To Heaven He ascended and unfolds the glad story,
The hosts of the blessed exult in His fame.
In love He looks down from the throne of His glory,
And rescues the ruined who trust in His name.
Sound the high praises of Jesus, the King!
He came and He conquered – His victory sing.

Thomas Moore

Daniel told Nebuchadnezzar about God's choice for a king.

"Whom He would He set up; and whom He would He put down" (Dan. 5:19).

Daniel was speaking to King Nebuchadnezzar and said,

"That the living may know that the Most High ruleth in the kingdom of men, and giveth it to whomsoever He will, and sitteth up over it the basest of men" (Dan. 4:17).

Separation from the World

Note: Daniel said that God has the option of setting the basest of men over the kingdom of men. There will be individuals in power whom we do not agree with and would prefer they were not in power. Let us run over a few names and say, "Would we have put them in power?" "Would we have voted for them and chosen them as world leaders in their time?" "Given a choice would we have given them a yes or no?" "Would we show our hands in approval for their selection?" If not, "Are we saying God made a mistake when He put them in power?" There can be no middle ground. Either God was right in His decisions, or He made a mistake. Even worse than that, those mistakes could have been avoided if we were there to correct them. We could have made choices that would have forestalled all of the terrible devastations that occurred in their countries. Some of them were the cause of terrible events as the Holocaust and multiple genocides and mass murders and carnage. The things men have done to men is inconceivable. "Were they only terrible mistakes?" "Could we have stopped them if we had the opportunity?"

In either case, let us start with:

1. Adolf Hitler
2. Joseph Stalin
3. Benito Mussolini
4. Vladimir Lenin
5. Saddam Hussein
6. Fidel Castro
7. Idi Amin Dada
8. Augusto Pinochet
9. Simon Bolivar
10. Francois Duvalier
11. Fulgencio Batista
12. Juan Peron.

As well as these and many others from recent years I have a list of some of the leaders in history whose rules were known for their cruelty

Joseph John Bowman

1. Genghis Khan killed approx. 11% of the world's population. He and his men raped and pillaged vast numbers of the remainder of the population of the earth. There is a gene common to Genghis Khan, and his sons found in up to 8% of those in Asia and 0.5% of the world's total.
2. Tamerlane the Great – He built towers out of the skulls of his enemies
3. Vlad the Impaler (aka Vlad Dracula) was famous for impaling his enemies
4. Qin Shi Huang (First Emperor of a unified Chinese Empire) He burned books and buried scholars alive (reportedly 460 Confucian scholars in one year). His massive works brought the nation to abject poverty.
5. Ivan IV – He killed his heir and watched countless of his people die of torture. He oversaw his first execution when only 13. He was known as Ivan the Terrible.
6. Leopold II was infamous for his inhumane treatment of residents of the Congo and those who were made slaves there. His men brutally raped the women and cut off the hands of living slaves to give proof to their superiors that they had not wasted valuable ammunition on them.
7. Pol Pot – was responsible for the deaths of over one-fifth of the population of Cambodia from executions and starvation.
8. Maximilien Robespierre – He was the French ruler during what became known as the Reign of Terror. He imprisoned approx. 300,000 and, killed roughly 40,000, many on the guillotine.
9. Mao Zedong – He founded the Peoples Republic of China. In 1957 he launched what became known as the Great Leap Forward. It led to the worse famine in history, and between 20-45 million people died between 1958-1962. Although there were significant developments during his reign, there were a massive number of deaths accountable to his rule. The numbers go from 30-70 million dead.

On top of these were all the Roman Emperors and Ceasars. There were the Pharaohs, and various Kings and Monarchs. As well, there

Separation from the World

are the rulers of various Arab nations both past and present. The list is endless. Were all these rulers merely aberrations or did God allow them? If God did, and Daniel 4:17 tells us that He did, what is our responsibility?

Do we accept them as rulers sent from God, or do we rebel? Do we say, as some do, that God allowed them to rule but did not want them in power? If we say that, we are saying while God allowed them into power, it was not according to His will. In that case, if we had been around, we could have stopped their evil actions and rule. If that is the case, we have more power and ability to stop the spread of evil in this world than Almighty God! We are giving ourselves the ability to enforce more important actions than can God Himself. Is it our duty to actively seek to see them dethroned and replaced?

If we are given that responsibility now why did God allow these godless individuals freedom to rule in days past? Why has He given us any more rights and privileges than He did to His people over the years? Have we been given an exclusive right and protection not afforded to the people of God over the ages? If so, why? What is so special about us that we do not need to obey and yield to the powers that be? If God demanded it of His people in the past, what makes us so special today? Are we that much more spiritual and valuable to the work of God that we can disregard His commands for us? Is He willing to overlook our disobedience because if He did not, He could not accomplish His work without us?

Before we answer, I want to give another Scripture quickly. It is from the apostle Paul. He was writing to believers in one of the wickedest cities in the known world. It was famous for its excesses and immoralities. Their cruelties exerted on the less powerful are well known.

Joseph John Bowman

Despite all this, Paul said,

> "Let every soul be subject unto the higher powers. For there is no power but of God: the powers that be are ordained of God. Whosoever, therefore, resisted the power, resisted the ordinance of God: and they that resist shall receive to themselves damnation. For rulers are not a terror to good works, but to the evil. Wilt thou then not be afraid of the power? Do that which is good, and thou shalt have praise of the same: for he is the minister of God to thee for good. But if thou do that which is evil, be afraid: for he beareth not the sword in vain: for he is the minister of God, a revenger to execute wrath upon him that doeth evil. Wherefore ye must needs be subject, not only for wrath, but also for conscience sake. For this cause pay ye tribute also: for they are God's ministers, attending continually upon this very thing. Render therefore to all their dues: tribute to whom tribute is due; custom to whom custom; fear to whom fear; honor to whom honor" (Rom. 13:1-7).

I could go on and on with these questions. However, I think we can all get the point I am trying to make. We are under an injunction to serve and please the God who redeemed us. It is He who has given us the commandments He wants us to keep. It is He who has promised to be with us through all the problems of life. Let us depend on Him in it all.

Is God in Control?

At the start of this section, let us read the words of the chorus of a hymn written by Kittie Suffield.

Separation from the World

"God Is Still on the Throne"

"God is still on the Throne,
And He will remember His own;
Tho' trials may press us and burdens distress us,
He never will leave us alone;
God is still on the Throne,
He never forsaketh His own;
His promise is true, He will not forget you,
God is still on the Throne."

Kittie Suffield

As we look at the question that starts this section, we need to ask the following question. "Is the One on the Throne in charge?" "Is He the one whom we are to obey?" Alternatively, "Is He like other earthly rulers needing the advice and direction of counselors and advocates?" "Do we have an important role to play in giving appropriate advice and counsel to the God of the Universe?" If so, "How did He manage before we came along?"

It is God, who establishes individuals into the positions of authority, and who removes them from it when their time is done. The responsibility and duty is not ours. We are apt to make mistakes. God will never make a mistake. We can and will show favoritism and preferences to one over another. We know, or we should, that God will choose individuals who will fulfill His will regardless of who they may be. That teaching, is essential, for, the option did not exist then, to vote a person out of, or into, office. We have no permission given to us, to rise in rebellion against established authority and power. No matter where we look for permission in the teachings to the Church, we cannot find it. It is God who instituted the government that is in power, despite any feelings we may have about how they are governing, irrespective of whether or not what they are doing is favorable to the work of God on earth.

Joseph John Bowman

I sought to give my mother an example as to why it is wrong to get involved in politics.

The example was dealing with the Canadian political situation of the time.

> "If there were an election today, each of us would vote differently. That said, each of us would be confident that we voted by the will of God. Some would vote Conservative as that is where their leanings take them. Many Saints have more of a tendency to vote for the Alliance Party. (Which, is now no longer in existence, as it is now part of, the Conservative Party of Canada.) The Alliance Party had some Christian roots and beliefs. (It is an interesting point of history that although Christians voted for the Alliance Party en mass, it never gained power in Canada. Power went to the other parties. (Except the NDP.) Some governments have proved to be good for the country, and others not so good. Despite it all, it was God who placed the parties and their leaders in power.) Some would vote for the Liberals, and there are always NDP sympathizers among us. There is now the Green Party. It is a party with growing support and power in Canada. In the end, there would be Christians who would vote for each of these parties. When asked, every one of them would state with conviction, that they had voted according to the revealed will of God for them. They would be insulted if there were any inference that God would have had them vote any other way. In the end, only one person will become the leader of the country. Only one party will hold the reins of power. In that case, every person who voted against him and his party voted against the will of God, for God put the person of His choice in power.

Separation from the World

Despite what we think, God does not need our input or interference. All He needs is our obedience. We are to be separate from all of the activities of this world. That includes the political world.

There is no other type of union that God has made His will more clearly known that His people separate from. He has clearly stated He is in control and overall. He alone can influence the decisions made by the governments of this world.

Some of the politicians involved in some of these parties profess to be Christians and hold Biblical stands. Some of these are things like abortion, homosexuality, gay marriage, and today, gender fluidity as well as the death penalty. They may also be against things that the Christian right adamantly opposes. When they come into the halls of power, they are either unable or unwilling to effect the changes that they promised. They come under the influence of the polls and opinions of the general population. It becomes evident that if they desire reelection, they need to cater to the will of the people. In the end, they were no better than those who went before them.

The majority of the governments of the day have been deficient morally. It is evident in the laws they have passed and the judgments made. The legal decisions of the courts of the land have been deplorable. Racism and lack of restraint are in our police departments. Lack of the ability to make the right judgments is common. Injustice and a lack of morals are in our courtrooms. Inequality and a lack of ethics and morals are found right up to the Supreme Court, the chief court of the land. That attitude permeates the justice systems from the lowest courts right to the Supreme Court. It is evident in our rulers. It matters not who they are. It may be our Prime Ministers or Presidents, our Kings, and Queens. The list is endless. There is a lack of moral clarity among them. It is in the actions of the various Members of Parliament.

Corruption is not only prevalent, but it is permitted. Wickedness has a place of exaltation. Anyone who has the temerity to speak against the evils of the day is put down and silenced. Names are smeared,

Joseph John Bowman

and reputations destroyed. (All this is the result of their stands on moral issues.) Unless it becomes a public scandal, the perpetrators are pardoned and excused. They have acted in ways by which they have shown the way they considered the ethics of the country. Some have even broken the laws of the land. They are guilty of crimes against humanity. Some are guilty of chemical warfare, even against their nations. Many have committed genocide and caused their people to die and suffer unspeakable horrors. Their attitudes have been worse than many who are now in the prisons of the land. Despite that, they are the rulers of the country.

An example is gay marriage. As well there are all of the different aspects of the LGBTQ communities. There is what is referred to in society as gender fluidity. There are no morals or purity between the sexes. It is allowed and encouraged by society and even the school systems in their younger years. These live styles have now all received legal recognition and acceptance. We acknowledge the wickedness and departure from God. The leaders who were responsible for these changes are put into power by God. If we believe otherwise, God is powerless to effect change on the earth.

We do not need to try to change the ways of men. The decisions they make and the programs they seek to encourage are beyond our ability to change. The ability of an unsaved man to worship God is futile. Humanities ways of seeking to find a way into God's presence will never work. Humanity always seeks to earn acceptance by their good works. They consider their money to be indispensable to the needs of humanity. They feel that there is something about them that is favorable in the sight of God. Something they do, and a charitable organization or work they give to or are involved in will win them favor with God.

God has stated His position very clearly. He does not need a man to fulfill His work. The best humanity can do is unworthy of entering into the presence of God.

Separation from the World

Nothing about us that is commendable in God's sight.

> "But we are all as an unclean thing, and all our righteousnesses are as filthy rags" (Is. 64:6).

We have not one thing we can bring to God that He needs. He is the possessor of all things. We are but His creation.

As a result, He said that He is not,

> "Worshipped with men's hands, as though He needed anything, seeing He giveth to all life and breath, and all things" (Acts 17:25).

Our God is not impressed with our might or power. Any riches we may accumulate is nothing compared to the wealth of Him Who is Almighty God.

He said to His people,

> "For every beast of the forest is Mine, and the cattle upon a thousand hills. I know all the fowls of the mountains: and the wild beats of the field are Mine. If I were hungry, I would not tell thee: for the world is mine, and the fulness thereof" (Ps. 50:10-12).

God is the possessor of all things. It is He who made them, and who controls their every action. There is nothing about them that is not under His control. Humanity seeks to separate themselves from the guiding hand of God. They act like they are independent of any responsibility towards the God who created them.

In this vein, read Luke 12:16-21. Read it carefully, especially if you are unsaved. The account is of a rich man. He had everything, even more than he could handle. He was going to expand his empire. He desired to build his domain without any acknowledgment to God. He

Joseph John Bowman

thought that he could manage something as small and insignificant as the matters of this earth!

Sadly, for him, we have the words of God;

> "Thou fool, this night thy soul shall be required of thee: then whose shall those things be, which thou hast provided? So is he that layeth up treasure for himself, and is not rich toward God" (Luke 12:20-21).

In everything we do and every decision, we make humanity must take God into their consideration. Unfortunately, many times, we seek to act independently from God and His will for us. This attitude is in every aspect of our lives, and no more so than in the political arena.

Those in power are not to be our concern. Everything in life is under God's control. We do not have to worry about the future. The rich man thought he had it all under his control. However, he forgot one little detail. God is overall. God whom the rich man forgot and did not take into account, had the final say.

In the plan of God, He has the final say over the affairs of this world. He is the One who has the authority to make the final decisions. He can determine what the right judgments should be. What valuable part do we feel we can play in the decisions of the Godhead? Would it not be far better to leave the decision with God? God has given us responsibility and a valuable part to play.

We are not to interfere with His decisions or choices

> "I exhort you, therefore, that first of all, supplications, prayers, intercessions, and giving of thanks, be made for all men; for kings, and for all that are in authority; that we may lead a quiet and peaceable life in all Godliness and honesty" (1 Tim.2:1-2).

Separation from the World

We are to pray for them, and their time in office instead of taking stands against them!

"Is there a more valuable work anyone can perform on earth?" "What position is of greater import than to take another human being before the Throne of Grace?" We have the privilege of representing our leaders before God. We are not to be found taking them before the courts of men. We are bringing them before the presence of the August Ruler of the universe. We should feel the awesome responsibility given to us. If we act in any way that shows that we feel we have a greater responsibility to act on earth we are saying that our actions on earth are of more importance that the power of the God of Heaven.

Looking at politicians as they campaign for votes, there is nothing that is God-honoring about the process. It is full of lies and false promises and insinuations. I recently heard a woman make a statement about a politician she admired. She said that there was nothing in his platform that she could believe. However, in the end, she said that she would vote for him because he always told the truth. It was a complete paradox. Either he was a liar, or everything he said was trustworthy. There is no middle ground.

Listen as they attack one another both personally as well as professionally. The desire is to seek to ruin the reputations of their opponents and to destroy them politically. It is not only their political destruction but the destruction of the families and the careers of those against whom they are running. They try to destroy the names and reputations of those who follow their opponents. They want to leave no man standing. It is all or nothing. A political leader recently said as a campaign was ongoing for a new government. "While they go low, we will go high." Almost immediately she said that her party started a smear campaign against the man they were opposing. After the election, a crusade began to destroy the winner. A political crusade was formed to ruin his reputation, character, and ability to govern. "Is, there anything that honors God or shows forth His love for humanity in this process?" There is not, and that is because every aspect of it is of this world, and is from the Wicked One!

Joseph John Bowman

By attempting to change things using our votes, we are seeking to do that which is impossible.

God in His Word said:

> "Things would wax (get – Ed.) worse and worse" (1 Tim. 3:15).

We need to do as David did when he saw how the wicked prospered. As he saw them, it seemed that they could do no wrong.

It was like King Midas:

> "Everything they touched turned to gold."

> "For I was envious at the foolish when I saw the prosperity of the wicked. For there are no bands (pains – Ed.) in their death: but their strength is firm. They are not in trouble as other men: neither are they plagued like other men. Therefore pride compasseth them about as a chain: violence covereth them as a garment. Their eyes stand out with fatness: they have more than heart could wish. They are corrupt, and speak wickedly concerning oppression: they speak loftily. They set their mouth against the heavens, and their tongue walketh through the earth. Therefore his people return hither: and waters of a full cup are wrung out to them. And they say, How doth God know? And is there knowledge in the Most High? Behold, these are the ungodly, who prosper in the world: they increase in riches" (Ps. 73:3-12).

The above words could describe any worldly corporation or government in this world. The people of this world are seeking their riches and power, without acknowledging the power of God. They refuse to acknowledge that there is One to whom they are accountable. Humanity desires to do what they want to whom they want and when

Separation from the World

they want. They will take no restrictions or restraints from anyone or anything other than themselves. They are seeking to place God to one side. In all their ways, they are trying to belittle God. He is considered only a minor nuisance to them. That was their opinion in the past, and it is their opinion today. David was not finished. He had a refuge and point of safety, and security the world does not have.

He went on to say,

> "When I thought to know this, it was too painful for me: until I went into the Sanctuary of God: then understood I their end. Surely Thou didst set them in slippery places: Thou castest them down into destruction. How are they brought into desolation, as in a moment! They are utterly consumed with terrors. As a dream when one awaketh: Thou shalt despise their image" (Ps. 73:16-20).

We, as David did, can rest assured we have a God who is in control. All the wicked can do is to ensure their judgment. The more they depart from God, the more severe it will be.

The Lord Jesus said about those who had more opportunity versus those who had little opportunity;

> "And thou, Capernaum, which art exalted unto Heaven, shalt be brought down to Hell: for if the mighty works, which have been done in thee, had been done in Sodom, it would have remained until this day. But I say unto you, that it shall be more tolerable for the land of Sodom in the day of judgment, than for thee"(Matt. 11:23-24).

It is important to note that our Lord did not say that the judgment that Sodom would face would be tolerable. There is no way we can fathom the horrors of God's judgment on those in Hell. It will be unfathomable! Despite that, there will be levels of judgment. He said the punishment

Joseph John Bowman

of Sodom and Gomorrha would be "more tolerable" than that which Capernaum would face. Capernaum had greater opportunities than Sodom. They had significantly more opportunities to receive the gift of God's salvation. Therefore, they would face greater judgment because of their rejection of the Saviour. The same thing can be said about each one of us today. We will be responsible before God according to the opportunities He has given us for our salvation. Along with that will be the wickedness in their lives. The Bible tells us that every aspect of an unbelievers life is in rebellion to the will of God.

We have no control over anyone's choices or responsibility to God. It is not our responsibility to place limits on their departure from God. God alone will say how far they can go without His intervening in their affairs.

Every believer must witness to this world about their sinfulness. Every person needs to be told that their lives are in rebellion to God. As a result of their rebellion, they will face God's judging hand. However, God has provided a way whereby they might be saved. The message is not only one of condemnation. It is one of hope and salvation. That is the meaning of the Gospel. The word means "Good News." God has a message of good news for sinful man. The duty we have is to spread that message to the whole world.

It matters not their position in society or government;

> "Who will have all men to saved, and to come unto
> the knowledge of the truth" (1 Tim. 2:4).

The only possibility for change is through the salvation of souls. It is not through changes in governments.

It was said of the apostle Paul and those who traveled with him when they arrived in Thessalonica,

> "These men who have turned the world upside down
> have come hither" (Acts 17:6).

136

Separation from the World

The early disciples did not attempt or encourage any political actions or insurrections against the government of the day. Rebellion is never countenanced, no matter how appalling the governments are in their decadence and wickedness. Christians today go on marches and sign petitions and attend rallies stating their disapproval of political stands on different things publicly. God has stated His hatred of the sins of humanity. Nowhere has He voiced His approval of any acts of defiance. Insurrection or disobedience against any God-ordained rule is wrong. We are not to be a rebel or rise in rebellion against any form of rule. The salvation of souls is the only way that man will see any change for good. We are never even given a hint that godly change can come into effect by changes in government. It is not changing the way we are ruled that is needed. The only change that counts are changes that take place in the heart. The only way for that to take place is through the new birth. We will then have a new nature and partake in a new life. Only then will any change that will be blessed by God take place.

The Believer's Responsibility on Earth

We have the words of the Apostle Paul in Romans 13:1-7. Paul is telling us to obey the powers that are in control since they are God-given. We know that all they do and say is by the permission of God who is in control. Therefore if we disobey, we are disobeying those whom God has placed over us. The reason they are in power is so that they will punish evildoers. (This is the mandate that God has given them. They are to be in the positions of power that they hold for the good of those under them. Nowhere are we exhorted that if they do not fulfill the dictate that God has given them, we are to rise in rebellion, and seek to see them replaced.) As, an example of this, none of the Apostles, advocated that the Christians were to in any way to resist the powers in Rome. Even though Rome abused its God-given position of power by persecuting and killing the Christians, an insurrection was not encouraged.

Joseph John Bowman

There was injustice seen in the Roman Empire. It is worthy of note that sin is not only currently found in our world and governments. We sometimes talk with longing about the "Good old days." It is unclear what is meant, for sin was equally prevalent in every age. Wickedness and rebellion against God is not a new phenomenon. It has existed since Adam and Eve took of the fruit in the Garden. Rebellion is part of the human psyche. It has existed throughout time. It will never end until He who is the Prince of Peace comes to rule over this world. Sin and their practices were equally, if not more evident in the Roman world. Gross immorality was prevalent, and the fact of homosexuality, even in the palace, was well known. Murders were commonplace, and there was a great dereliction of responsibility towards those whom they had under them. The issue of the treatment of slaves and the fact of slavery itself is well known. Slavery was not condemned, nor were believers encouraged to stand against it.

All of the sins of the day were condemned. No believer was to take part in them during their daily lives. However, no believer was even encouraged to take a public stand against these sins and those who committed them. Sin was condemned in all its wickedness, yet the believers were not taught that they were to be instruments of change for society.

Christian slave owners were to treat their slaves (employees) in a Godly manner. A Christian master did not have the same freedom to treat his slaves in an inhumane manner as their unsaved contemporaries. (See Paul returning Onesimus to Philemon in the little book of Philemon.) In various other places, slaves were told to be obedient to their masters. At the same time, the master was exhorted to treat their slaves in a fair, humane manner. It was to be so that those would see how their testimonies practically affected their everyday lives.

There was the almost sub-human treatment of women and other minorities. Women were treated as sex objects and were for the entertainment of those over them. The various Ceasars were famous for their sexual tendencies. All they had to do was to make known their desire for their immoral associations with any of the women.

Separation from the World

It extended to the wives and consorts of the senators and governors in Rome. They were considered no better than playthings of their husbands and overlords.

Most of those who were minorities in Rome served as slaves. Their degrees of subjection went from an ordinary household slave to one who had a position of leadership over a large portion of their master's estate.

Some of them trained as gladiators. They battled to the death in arenas around the Roman empire. No matter how important they were to their masters, their end was the same. They were all offered up in death in their various contests. Some of these were against other gladiators while others were against wild beasts. The reason for these activities was to provide entertainment for the masses. Their final deaths provided the people with a morbid measure of satisfaction.

There were many gross cases of abuse of power by Rome and the other governments of the day as well as many terrible instances of immorality. It is a fact of history that the primary sin that caused the decline and downfall of the majority of the great empires of years past was immorality. Archeologists and paleo archeologists witnessed the lack of morals in their examinations of ancient cultures and ruins. Immorality was rampant among the cultures of the past. It did not matter how cultured and what degree of sophistication they had. They were all marked by both idolatry and the immorality that went along with it. Sexual deviancies were practiced in their immoral lifestyle with young children. It was what we call paedifillia today and included both boys and girls. It was seen in the offerings of virgins to their gods and the sexual practices that took place in their temples. Nothing they desired was held back from them.

There is a saying

"If you do not learn from history, you will repeat it."

All of the great civilizations of this world need to take heed. They are fast following the failures that marked those who fell in the past. We,

Joseph John Bowman

as believers, are powerless to stop the march of nations. We are here to seek to slow the march of souls to the Pit of Hell. Those are they we are to seek to see changed. It will be through their salvation, change will be wrought. While their change may affect society, it is first to be in their hearts. Next, the actions of their lives will be evident. Finally, change may be among those the believer's contact. Changes will not occur through any amount of good works or cultural or environmental improvements. It matters not a whit if the environment or oceans are clean if men's hearts are defiled. We are not here to improve society. Our efforts are to be Godly testimonies to those around us. Only then will any changes be affected.

The Christians were not told to fight against the processes, good or evil. They were told to remain separate from them all.

> "Wherefore come out from among them, and be ye separate, saith the Lord, and touch not the unclean thing: and I will receive you, and will be a Father unto you, and ye shall be My sons and daughters, saith the Lord Almighty" (2 Cor.6:17-18).

We, are not placed on earth to affect the betterment of humanity, but, that they might be saved, and brought to God. Then, and only then, will there be a change that will last! The change that will occur will never end, not only now but for eternity. It will affect the destination of a soul from death to life. The soul will change destinations from the Pit of Hell to the glories of Heaven. Is this change not worth our effort? Should we not strive for it in our lives?

As we see, in all these things, we are to submit to our rulers and pray for them and their salvation.

> "I exhort therefore, that, first of all, supplications, prayers, intercessions, and giving of thanks, be made for all men; for Kings, and for all that are in authority; that we may lead a quiet and peaceable life in all Godliness and honesty" (1 Tim. 2:1-2).

Separation from the World

There is not one word in this verse about our praying, let alone acting in rebellion against those in authority. We are to pray for our leaders and not against them. We are to pray for them as they govern us. We are exhorted to intercede before the Throne of God for them. Not only so, but we are also to give God thanks for them. There was not even a hint that if the believers were not able to live quiet and peaceable lives, they were to lead an insurrection. They were under an injunction to continue praying — in whatever circumstances they may find themselves. We are to pray for their salvation as we would for all humanity. The aim of our prayers is that we are to ask God that the people of God could live their lives in peace and quietness. We are to pray that the rulers will allow us to live Godly, quiet lives. Amid our lives, we are not encouraged to break the peace God has given by acts of defiance. We are not to start a revolution or take part in the same. We should never have a reputation as those who are revolting against the government of the day. Our lives are not to be marred by taking part in marches or rebellions either peaceable or semi-violent. The whole concept of believers acting in this way is wholly foreign to the Word of God.

The only time when we are permitted to disobey the governments of the day is when their unequivocal commands bring us into direct disobedience with the Word to God.

Our obedience is to be unto Him;

> "Did not we straitly command you that ye should not teach in this name? And, behold, ye have filled Jerusalem with your doctrine, and intend to bring this man's blood upon us. Then Peter and the apostles answered and said, We ought to obey God rather than men" (Acts 5:28-29).

Their response was that which showed their obedience and dedication to God.

Joseph John Bowman

By so saying the believers were firmly placing their flag of allegiance before the cross of Christ. Even though they did, so they never sought to remove or replace Rome or the Roman governors or rulers. They obeyed them in every way that they could without disobeying the commands of their Lord. They never sought to lead an insurrection against Rome. They never encouraged the populace of the cities they entered to rebel. Their message to the citizens of the cities they went to was straightforward. It was repentance towards God and faith in our Lord Jesus Christ (Acts 20:21). It was only then that change would be affected. It was only to those who believed that change evidenced itself. It was only the changes in the lives of believers that evidenced itself to such an extent that it was said that they turned the world upside down (Acts 17:6). Any unsaved personal who sought to number themselves with the believers were discouraged and sent away.

Peter said the following to those who by becoming part of them sought to make money.

> "But Peter said unto him, thy money perish with thee, because thou hast thought that the gift of God may be purchased with money. Thou hast neither part nor lot in this matter: for thy heart is not right in the sight of God. Repent therefore of this thy wickedness, and pray God, if perhaps the thought of thine heart may be forgiven thee" (Acts 8:20-22).

God moved in judgment about the situation around Ananias and Sapphira, his wife. As a result, the fear of God entered into the multitude.

Because of the evidence of the judging hand of God:

> "Of the rest durst no man to join himself to them: but the people magnified them" (Acts 5:13).

We are to be separate from this world. The world should see that there is a difference. By witnessing our separation to our God, they

Separation from the World

will glorify God. They will do so even when they act in hatred and rebellion to Him and His will.

The believers were to seek to see the unbelievers of this world saved. Our object is not to better their lives. It does not matter whether a sinner lives a better life morally, or in any other way if they die in their sins. They will still go to Hell even though they may have lived an upwardly moral life.

We need to be very careful about how we follow this exhortation to disobey the commands of our local governments. Some say that anything we disagree with will fall under this dictate. Others say that it includes anything that disagrees with the commands of God for humanity. Many believers will state that this statement gives us the freedom to go on marches and in any other way to signify our opposition to ungodly stands by our leaders. By holding this position, we are permitted to live and act in a continual state of hostility resisting the laws of the different forms of government we have. We can take part in actions of civil disobedience as well as seeking to make our stands take a prominent place on social media. By doing this, we can ruin the reputation and lifestyle of those we attack.

It includes online bullying, which is illegal in many countries. It has been the cause of numerous individuals, especially young people committing suicide. Another word used is that an individual has been doxed.

A definition of what doxing means is:

> "To make public all of the private information that can be found out about the individual."

It is a major desecration of the privacy of any person. It can set them up for any manner of social bullying and abuse. It can even end up in being the cause of physical abuse to the person. Even the terms used should signify that they are inconsistent with the way a child of God should act. Opposition is enacted in our boycotting both the government, as well as different companies and corporations that

Joseph John Bowman

identify themselves with the stands we oppose. It can be the reason for some companies going out of business or losing business. As a result, employees can lose their jobs, and it can be the cause of a significant downturn in the economy. "Should Christians to be involved in any of these activities?"

In today's society showing our opposition and the way we feel about governmental decisions can be shown not only through active measures like going on marches and displaying our displeasure against their stands publicly. There is also the use of social media. It is an area we need to be very careful about how we express ourselves. There is a danger that we will lose control over our comments and thoughts when we feel we have a degree of being anonymous. It can cause a believer to say things and make threats for which they may face criminal charges. That would be inconsistent with the life and testimony of any follower of the Lord. If we become too aggressive, it can be called online bullying and become the cause of a person losing their reputation and even their jobs and causing family problems. In the end, problems caused by social media can go to the extent of some individuals taking their lives. Suicide and depression are significant problems caused by individuals losing everything as a result of the excessive detrimental publication of private personal information. Many sources go back years into a persons life and find many negative aspects regarding them. They then use these factors to seek to ruin the individual's lives and reputations. At the end of this section, I want only to ask each of us; "Is this the activity we want to be found doing?" "Do we feel that God would have us ruin someone's reputation and maybe cause them irreparable harm?" "Is this how we are to fulfill the commandment our Lord gave us?"

The greatest commandment was;

> "Thou shalt love the Lord thy God with all thy heart, and with all thy soul, and with all thy mind. This is the first and great commandment. And the second is like unto it, thou shalt love thy neighbor as thyself" (Matt. 22:37-39.

Separation from the World

"Can we honestly, say, before God, that our attempts to ruin a persons reputation and life is the way God would have us show love to our neighbor?" "Is there no more practical way we can show how much we love those around us?" "Can we honestly say that God would have us sink to the level of those around us to fulfill His will?" "Are we no better than the world from which we are exhorted to be separated?" "Do we want to be identified with those who hate our Lord?" Watching marches and demonstrations; what we see portrayed are anger and hatred. "By this is the love of God portrayed to all around?" "As we listen to the words and actions of those who are the leaders of these demonstrations, and the hatred they spew forth, "Is this the way we want to express ourselves?" " Can we say that these activities would be that which would identify the activities of our Lord if He was here on earth?" "Is this the way God showed His love for us?" "Are we able to spread the love of God to those around as we take part in these activities?" "Does our participation in any way mar our testimonies for God?" We need to remember that before God saved us, we were enemies and living in enmity to God. God, who could have eternally condemned us, and sent us to Hell, offered us His salvation. He saved us from much worse than we can ever imagine. "Can we say that despite what those around us are guilty of, that our God does not desire to see them saved?"

The justification we use to engage in all of these activities is that we are doing them in the name of God. We say that these activities show our obedience to the commands of God for us. We are therefore acceding to the wishes of God for His people. By extension, we are applying these wishes to the world around us. We say that we are therefore living lives before this world showing the moral character of God. By our lives, we say that the world sees the person of God in us and our acts.

In its context, the only time we are permitted to disobey the authorities is when their commands bring us directly in opposition to the Word and will of God. Therefore it must affect us as believers directly, and not just have an indirect action on our lives. The fact that it directly refers to the world has nothing to do with our stand before God. God

145

Joseph John Bowman

will judge this world in His way, and through the standards He has set. We are not responsible for setting the moral stands of this world. We are personally responsible for maintaining an ethical manner of life. We have no responsibility to force the world to live the life of a child of God. We are under an exhortation to condemn their lifestyle. The way this world lives is not our responsibility. Our work before God is to live righteous lives before Him. It is not to force this world to live under the law of God. We are to bring the love and righteous requirements of God before them. The way we do that is to present the Gospel of the Grace of God to them. We are to seek to see them saved. Their lives will be changed from the dead things of this world to that of the life of God. That is the only way that God expects this world to change in their moral or ethical character before Him. The salvation of souls is the only way God will recognize any changes made in this world.

Anything else falls under the auspices of good works.

> "Not by works of righteousness which we have done,
> but according to His mercy, He saved us" (Titus 3:5).

Again:

> "But we are all as an unclean thing, and all our
> righteousnesses are as filthy rags: and we all do fade
> as a leaf: and our iniquities, like the wind, have taken
> us away" (Is. 64:6).

Good works will never save us or gain us favor with God. We are never exhorted to seek to make the world a better place. We are not to improve the world's standard of living or ensure that the inhabitants have a better place to live. We must show men that they are sinners and condemned by God. By accepting their condition, they will then be in a state whereby a holy God can save them. Otherwise, they will think they are too holy to need God's salvation. They will depend on their good works to gain the favor of God.

146

Separation from the World

Although the world has legalized abortion, there is no necessity that a believer follows the law and does it. If such were the case, then we would have a Scriptural reason to stand against it personally. That personal stand would not justify going on marches seeking to abolish it in the world. The same stand goes for same-sex marriages and relationships. I have mentioned already in this book the ongoing push for what is called gender fluidity. It would be impossible to mention all of the sexual sins and departures from the will and Word of God. If God's plan for us as His people were to march and go on demonstrations every time this world deviated from the plan of God, we would be doing nothing else.

If the time ever comes when believers are expected to perform these marriages (same-sex or other types than between a man and a woman) or accept them into the fellowship of the local gathering, then we would be right to stand against that law personally and corporately. It may be that those among us who are in the medical profession will be called to perform abortions. It may be that we will have to take a public, yet private stand against this sin. By so doing it may cost the believer their livelihood and maybe even more. There are more points than we can mention. We cannot go into all of the rampant types of immorality there are in this world. As well, there are things like alcohol abuses and gambling meccas. Drug use is legalized in many places. When we view the sin of prostitution, we cannot ignore the evil of pornography.

Along with that comes sexual slavery and sex videos and the different types of sexual abuse. We cannot begin to state all of the illegal and unethical things that go on in business and politics. It will never end, and we can never stop finding issues we will disagree with and want to take stands against wherever we are. "Where will it all end?" "What is most important?" "Is it to take a public stand against these sins or to take a stand for the person of our Lord Jesus Christ?" "Are we exhorted to cleanse this world or to be witnesses to it?" We are nowhere expected to resist actively but to take a decided passive stand. That will allow us to keep our Scriptural stands as well as a testimony before the world.

Joseph John Bowman

There was just a bylaw passed by the city of Berkley, California. It states that the city is now gender-neutral. It has now banned every type of gender-specific language.

The ordinance passed states:

> "In recent years, broadening societal awareness of transgender and gender-nonconforming identities has brought to light the importance of non-binary gender inclusivity."

> There are those today who are identified as having a non-binary gender. It is known as genderqueer and is a spectrum of gender identities that are not exclusively male or female. A non-binary person may claim to have more than one gender or to have no gender. They may even claim that they now have a third gender. It has been suggested that there are as many as 81 different gender types."

It is an abomination before the Lord; Paul wrote:

> "For this cause, God gave them up unto vile affections: for even their women did change the natural use into that which is against nature: and likewise also the men, leaving the natural use of the woman, burned in lust one toward another; men with men working that which is unseemly, and receiving in themselves the recompense of their error which was meet" (Rom. 1:26-27).

We need to recognize that the whole world is godless. The inhabitants of it are going to live in a godless manner and are going to a godless eternity. We cannot expect any better of this world. Our primary dictate is to seek to see the lost in the world saved. Salvation will change them from the children of darkness, into the children of light. Their salvation alone can make the changes necessary to please a holy

Separation from the World

God. If there is no change, we have a right to question their salvation. In all of this, we need to keep in mind that the whole world lieth in wickedness (1 John 5:19).

The world dwells in darkness and is ruled by the prince of darkness, the Devil. He is the one who is leading the children of this world in the paths of wickedness. It is his guidance that is causing the leaders we are under to go in sinful ways.

(We are to pray for and not against the rulers of this world. We are not to try to see them be replaced or removed from power. When we pray for someone, we have their best interests at heart. Our prayers that all of the world's leaders should first and foremost come to know the Lord Jesus as their personal Saviour.)

After that that they will allow us to live Godly lives peaceably here on earth.

Our aim on earth is to live:

> "A quiet and peaceable life in all godliness and honesty" (1 Tim. 2:2).

As we do, we will be able to be a testimony for Him with everyone, from the poorest to the most celebrated individual on the face of this earth. That is God's desire for us.

Our Responsibility – To the Union

The same principle of leaving governments in the hands of God should govern how we act, or react, our contacts at work. (That is union or non-union contracts.) We believe that God is in control of the governments of the day. (federal, provincial and municipal as well as our unions.) "Is He not watching over us?" "Does He not have a concern over how much we make as well as what benefits we receive?" The Lord Jesus, speaking of His care for us, was very

Joseph John Bowman

explicit. He told His disciples of His care for the things of nature. Beautiful though they are, they exist but for a moment and then are gone forever. At most, they are fleeting in existence. The God who created them has their interests at heart. He cares for them, although they are unaware of their needs. On their own, they are unable to look after themselves.

They are entirely dependant on the care of God.

> "If God so clothe the grass, which is today in the field, and tomorrow is cast into the oven; how much more will He clothe you, O ye of little faith?" (Luke 12:28).

Indeed, how much more will He clothe us?

Another passage that tells us of the care of our Heavenly Father for us is in the following verses.

> "Are not two sparrows sold for a farthing? And one of them shall not fall on the ground without your Father" (Matt.10:29).

He then said dealing with the same subject,

> "Are not five sparrows sold for two farthings, and not one of them is forgotten before God?" (Luke 12:6).

In that day a sparrow was of so little worth that if four were bought, one was thrown in free. The farthing was the smallest of the Roman coins. Two of them would be almost equal to a penny in our times. That valuation shows mans' estimation of a sparrow. God observed them so intently He knew when one of them fell to the earth. Amongst all of them, and they number in the millions, God forgot not one. The question we all need to ask is, "If God is so conscious of the needs of a sparrow, why do we feel He will forget us?"

Separation from the World

Our Lord went on to say,

> "But even the very hairs of your head are all numbered. Fear not, therefore: ye are of more value than many sparrows." (Luke 12:7).

God has given a number to each hair on our heads. He is so conscious of our needs. He is aware of our slightest change or cares we may have. Even the loss of a single hair is recorded in the Book of God.

The Psalmist tells us of the care He has for us:

> "Thou tellest all my wanderings: put Thou my tears into Thy bottle: are they not in Thy book?" (Ps.56:8).

He knows every step we take. We may think that no one cares when we sorrow. We may weep all alone and without anyone to care for us. There may be no one to pity or soothe us in our sorrows. There is One Who has kept every tear we ever wept in His bottle. He has such care for us that our tears are precious in His sight. They are not here one moment and then gone forever. Almighty God has kept every single one of them in His bottle. The tears of His people are so valuable that He will not allow a single one to be lost. Almighty God has written a book about them. He is aware of every situation we have gone through in our walk here below and knows any pain or sorrow and sadness or loss. He has a record of them all. "Why do we need to think that we need to concern ourselves with the affairs of this life?" He has kept a record of every step we have ever taken. He is in control of everything along the way. "Do we think we can do a better job of ordering our steps than He has?" "Are we more able to make more informed decisions about this life than Him?" He Who is our Counsellor and Comforter has everything under His control. His care for us is incomprehensible! "How dare we think that He will allow any evil thing to enter into our life without His permission?" He knows all about us. "How can we think we can order our steps more acceptably than the pathway He has chosen for us?"

Joseph John Bowman

The shame of it is many Christians vote their contracts and may even get involved in contract and labor negotiations. Some go even to the point of becoming a shop steward or union representative. Some will even find themselves in the union's executive branch. We must remember that we are not members of the local brotherhood, as they call it. Despite what they may say they are in it only for what they can get out of it, not for any real care for any of us.

They will call us their brothers or sisters in the union guild in which we are members. However, the majority of them will seek to put us down and even destroy our reputation and work record if it would serve them well. They may say they love us, their acts will destroy us if we do not back them in whatever plans they may have for the union and ultimately for their betterment. In the end, even if they seek our betterment, they desire that the management of the companies we may work for will be affected. It matters little to the union if the settlement they have forced on the company will cause it hardship in the future. All that matters is that the membership is enriched. They seek their welfare, not the welfare of others. Their whole way of life and the motives that drive them are opposed to that of believers.

We are taught to love one another. The first instance of love we see is the love of God for the world. The desire of God was not to condemn the world. It was to show His love to a lost world. That is the attitude we should show to those around us. It is not to be an attitude of rebellion and insubordination. That very thought is against the teachings of Scripture. It was not seen in the example of our Lord while here on earth. It should not be seen in us.

I want to ask a question at this point. "How can our witness be accepted if the individuals know that we have stood up against them?" We, as believers, have a duty and responsibility to be a witness not only to those we work with but towards those who employ us as well. We are to obey our employer unless it directly contravenes the Word of God.

Separation from the World

We are to submit and serve them as we would, the Lord.

> "Servants, obey in all things your masters according
> to the flesh: not with eyeservice, as men-pleasers: but
> in singleness of heart, fearing God: and whatsoever
> you do, do it heartily, as to the Lord, and not unto men:
> knowing that of the Lord ye shall receive the reward
> of the inheritance: for ye serve the Lord Christ" (Col.
> 3:22-24).

A point that needs mentioning is that some Christians spend company
time witnessing to their workmates. It is a means of theft. By doing
so, we are stealing time from our employers. Even if they do not say
anything, it will be noticed. The result of it will be that that the name
of our Lord will be blasphemed. We will lose our testimony among
them.

We may voice Scriptural opinions to them privately. Paul told us that
our witness is to be faithful in its aim. We are not to sugarcoat the
gospel as some do.

The apostle Paul said as he reviewed his life,

> "Wherefore, I take you to record this day, that I am
> pure from the blood of all men. For I have not shunned
> to declare unto you all the counsel of God" (Acts
> 20:26-27).

The exhortation for us is that we are to,

> "Let your speech always be with grace, seasoned with
> salt" (Col. 4:6).

I fear that there may be too much grace, and we compromise essential
truths. Either that, or there will be too much salt, and their response
will be to shun us. We need to be so careful that there is a godly
balance in our testimonies for Him, as we live below. They should

153

Joseph John Bowman

never be able to speak against us because of the stand that we have taken dealing with what we may hold on a personal or company relationship. Our position should be about the holiness of God and not the needs of man.

Paul told us,

> "Let your moderation be known unto all men. The
> Lord is at hand" (Phil 4:5).

Another way of putting that verse is that we are to let the sweetness of our reasonable nature be known unto all. That attitude is to be seen not only when we agree, but when we are judging an action of another. We are to have a fair and reasonable stand on all of these things. That is the teaching in this verse. The reason is that the Lord is standing at our right hand, observing everything we do and say. We need to keep in mind that we are always in the presence of God. The knowledge of the presence of God is to support every stand we take, whether it is in love or judgment.

We may have to join a union and pay dues to get work. Union membership is no more a partnership than possessing a Safeway Club Card makes the possessor a partner with Safeway. There is a marked difference between a relationship and one that becomes a partnership. In John 17:17-21, the Lord Jesus, while praying for His disciples, says that even though they were in this world, they are not of it. His prayer was that they would be preserved from the evil that is in it. He goes on to say that their responsibility is to represent Him. We do not become a partner with the world until we become involved with what they do, and are tied in with their systems.

We are not to get involved with the wrangling and infighting that goes on in union shops. By so doing, we are entering into a partnership with them. While they call themselves union brothers and sisters, there is no true fellowship there. They, would cut you off, or stab you in the back, (figuratively speaking) if it was to their advantage. Keep this in mind while working and associating with them.

154

Separation from the World

John said, in counter-distinction to what we see daily in the world:

> "That ye may have fellowship with us: and truly our fellowship is with the Father, and with His Son Jesus Christ" (1 John 1:3).

It is the only place where true fellowship abides.

We may try to excuse actions involving the union by saying it is our responsibility. The Bible teaches that our first responsibility is to God and the brethren. We are to act as the witnesses of God to the wicked, condemned, corrupt world. Some also try to excuse involvement by saying that it is an opportunity and freedom given to us. We ought to avail ourselves of it and make use of it. We may have to belong to a union to work; we have not the freedom of availing ourselves of every legal right that this world has to offer. The world and its leaders are godless. Every believer has a higher calling. There are many freedoms offered to the citizens of this world that are forbidden to the people of God. Because the world is allowed a privilege is no excuse for a believer to be taking part in it. We need to be able to discern what is of God and what is of the Evil One in this world.

The Alcoholics Anonymous prayer starts with the following words:

> "God grant me the Serenity, to accept the things I can not change, Courage to change the things I can, and the Wisdom to know the difference."

(One example of this is, that in most countries in this world, abortion is legal. They state that every woman has both a moral as well as a legal right to avail herself of this freedom. Liberal thinkers will say it an indication of a woman's feminity. By allowing it, we are told that a woman has the right to do what she will with her own body. No one else has the power or authority to tell her what she can or cannot do. It is not only a right; it has now almost become an obligation if a woman is to maintain her position in this world. Even those who do not practice it are obliged to voice their approval of this sin.

Joseph John Bowman

While society has given a woman this right, it would be wrong for a Christian sister to avail herself of it.

There is gay marriage among many other things. Humanity is forced to acknowledge multiple genders. I recently read that the State of California has now acknowledged 15 genders. Multi sex or gender-neutral washrooms are frequent, even in schools and other publicly used buildings. There recently was a bike ride in the city of Chicago called Dare to Bare. Participants wore little or no clothing. It was performed on the public streets in Chicago. Everyone who was there came into full view of the participants. Little children were exposed to their lewd actions. At the same time, Gay Parades are in almost every major city. Dress or the lack of it is typical. It provokes almost no comment anymore. Some places are now denied the right of using male and female pronouns. Words with masculine inference are now banned. Any words, called trigger words are avoided.

However, we are not to entangle ourselves with all of the social and political intricacies of these and other social problems in this world. The same principle applies here as well as in other areas of our lives.)

The rights we have are secure in Heaven, where they will never end or be changed, unlike on earth where they are subject to change. They are not dependent upon the whims of man but upon the unchanging Word of God. Let our lives be marked by the security we have. The world, as they look upon us, should see that we are different from them.

The Servant Master Relationship

Some go even further into the world of union involvement. They have become union representatives and shop stewards. Some may even be on the union executive. By becoming a union rep or shop steward, we will find ourselves standing on behalf of wicked men seeking to get away with as much as they can in opposition to their masters.

Separation from the World

It will bring us up against our masters or employers. They legitimately have the right to expect that we give them all that we can in our service to them.

Paul tells us what our attitude towards our employers should be. As we say this and take these stands, the world cannot understand the position that we take.

It is encapsulated in the following verses.

> "Servants, obey in all things your masters according to the flesh; not with eye service as men-pleasers; but with singleness of heart, fearing God: and whatsoever ye do, do it heartily, as unto the Lord, and not unto men; knowing that of the Lord ye shall receive the reward of the inheritance: for ye serve the Lord Christ"(Col. 3:22-24).

Union involvement will bring us against our masters in a confrontational manner. They have every right to expect that we give them all that we can in our service for them. They have hired us for our abilities and expertise. We are being paid to perform the duties they assign to us. We are under their employ. We are responsible for serving them faithfully. They are not responsible or subservient to us. If they know we are believers, and they should, it will be a terrible testimony before them. The unsaved have a greater understanding of the actions demanded of believers than many Christians have.

In our representation of fellow employees, we may very well be called upon to stretch the truth. Either that or we may not tell all of the pertinent facts relating to an incident. We may give them an unrealistic slant to make the one whose part we are representing look good. In all things, there are both the sins of omission as well as the sins of commission. Both are in evidence in a case like the one before us. We may even feel forced to tell outright lies, to fulfill the position and duties that we have. "What kind of impact will this have on our testimony among the unsaved, our bosses included?"

157

Joseph John Bowman

Our attitude to our masters, godless though they are to be,

> "Servants, be subject to your masters with all fear; not
> only to the good and gentle, but also to the froward
> (perverse; crooked – Ed.)" (1 Pet. 2:18).

That means that we are to be obedient to those who are disagreeable
and unreasonable as well as those who are kind to us. It is nothing
extraordinary to be agreeable to a kind boss. That is expected. What
is a source of wonder to this world is when we serve a boss who is
unreasonable in a manner that is not rebellious.

> "For what glory is it if, when ye be buffeted for your
> faults, ye shall take it patiently? But if, ye do well, and
> suffer for it, ye take it patiently, this is acceptable with
> God" (1 Pet. 2:20).

We will get no praise from God when we are punished for wrongdoing.
That is expected because we deserve the punishment we will get. We
have broken some rule or done something wrong. We can only expect
punishment. We are required to bear that patiently and not grieve it
to the union. We are not to try to get out of a deserved punishment.

Verse 20 goes on to say if we suffer wrongly and bear it patiently that
God will recognize it and reward us for it. There would be nothing
to recognize if we grieved it to the union and fought the charge. We
would have lost the reward of God whether or not we won or lost the
grievance. We need to recognize that in this world, we have no rights
except what God has given us. Seeking to see wrongs done against
us rectified is not one of them. The only exception would be if the
correction would remove reproach from the name of Christ. Even in
that case, we need to be careful that we do not go ahead of God in
this manner. God has His ways and means to justify His people. That
is both before the world as well as before His people.

Much less are we enjoined to represent another in opposition to our
masters or employers. We are not to rise in rebellion against our boss

Separation from the World

if they make things disagreeable for us. If we do so, how will we ever be able to witness to them? We do want to see them saved, do we not?

(Paul sent Onesimus back to Philemon that he might serve him forever. Onesimus was not told that his service was to change or made more comfortable. Philemon, in receiving Onesimus back received him as a brother in the Lord even though he resumed his service with Philemon once again.) (Read the Epistle of Paul to Philemon.)

The principles in these and other verses carry through to this day. In the days of the New Testament, it was a master-slave relationship. These same standards are placed upon us today. Then, as now, slaves tried to get away with as little work, or output as they could. They stole from their masters, time as well as material possessions. They misrepresented their masters in many different ways if they thought that they could get away with it. We, face these same problems, and many more, in the workforce today. I know that because I was part of the workforce. We are under the injunctions of Scripture to give our masters outstanding service. It may mean that we go further than our worldly associates in trying to please our masters. It may cause a personal problem. However, we are under the command to serve our masters to the best of our ability. We need to bear this in mind. What a disgrace it would be to the name of Christ if we had the reputation of getting away with as much as we could. It would be a disgrace to our testimonies if our fellow workers could say that we were lazy or dishonest or deceitful. If such were the case, then our testimonies among them would come to naught. Our lives at work should be such that all can see Christ in us. That is, even though they will persecute us.

I will end this part with the thought that we are on this earth to see Christ brought before an evil, dying world. Our purpose is to see them saved, not to better their living conditions. That applies to every aspect of life, as many try to do this in different aspects of the world today. Many, religions are involved in charitable organizations and movements in the world. They have become very well known for their activities in this way. However, it has affected their testimonies

Joseph John Bowman

in the gospel. That is because their desire now is to see humanity's living conditions bettered. Unfortunately, they often do this at the expense of their gospel testimonies. We have one responsibility laid on us in this world.

It is to be a witness to those around us and to proclaim the gospel of God to them.

> "For though I preach the gospel, I have nothing to
> glory of: for necessity is laid upon me; yea woe is me,
> if I preach not the gospel" (I Cor. 9:16).

It is the reason we are in this world. We are to be a testimony to unbelievers. As well we are to be an example of believers in our lives. It is evidenced before both the world, as well as other believers. If this is so, we should live up to its' aims and expectations.

In closing this section, I want to state that it is God who is going to judge us for our actions and not man. We find this truth brought out very clearly in the following verse,

> "For what glory is it, if, when ye be buffeted for your
> faults, (sins – Strong's) ye take it patiently? But if
> when ye do well, and suffer for it, ye take it patiently,
> this is acceptable with God" (1 Pet. 2:20).

I have previously covered most of the verse. I want to deal with the last word. That is the name of God. The Greek word used is "Theos," and the meaning is of the Supreme Divinity, by implication, a magistrate. This title is telling us of the One who is going to judge us. He is the One who is in control. He is the Supreme One who is one day going to be our magistrate. He is the One to whom we will answer. We need to keep this in our minds in all of our activities. That is over and above the fact that, in this earth, we are responsible to many earthly bosses and magistrates. Not all of them will be fair, however, the One before whom we have to do will be entirely fair and just. No one will ever be able to lay any charge of being partial

Separation from the World

or prejudiced against Him. For, He is the eternal Judge, who will have the final word on everything. He is the One who is going to judge us and, so we ought to live in the good of His judgment.

The Responsibility of Christian Employers

The above-given comments in no way relieve Christian employees from their God-given responsibilities to treat their employees fairly. If they treat them unfairly it will bring reproach upon the name of Christ. I remember one believer whom I knew quite well who made it very clear that he never took his Christian beliefs to work. I knew a brother who was well-known in both the world and in business for fraudulent activities. The way he cheated those he dealt with was common knowledge. Some believers go into debt and as a result, go into bankruptcy court. While it may be unavoidable in some instances, we need to ensure that it is not because of our fraudulent activities. Our Godly lives and testimonies should be evident to all around. In the gatherings of the local Church, we should be known as men and women of God.

I have known Christian employers who had a reputation of being nearly impossible to serve. Some of their employees voiced their frustrations verbally. Other employers were taken to court. Sometimes they were sued to force them to pay their bills. Other times complaints were lodged with the local chapters of the Employee Assistance Program. Numerous organizations represent workers in this way. Some are governmental, and some are private. They all serve the purpose of representing any worker who has had unfair or unrealistic expectations placed on them. Some employees even asked to work in unsafe conditions. Bosses may take liberties in their employee's personal lives and habits. All of these items and more are subject to infringement of human rights and the employment codes of health and safety. It should never be reported that a believer is forcing an employee to work in unsafe conditions. Either that or to work in a situation where either they or another person may be hurt or killed. That would be a terrible indictment against any child of God.

Joseph John Bowman

Sometimes, work that they expect is not reasonable, and other times they have unreal work expectations from their employees. Unfortunately, there have been numerous Christian employers who have the reputation of not paying their workers adequately. I once heard of a Christian boss who always paid his debts late and had his staff working in sub-par conditions. A reason for these actions may be that the boss can gain more income while in control of the funds (interest payments, etcetera). I have heard individuals, both saved and unsaved, state emphatically that they would never work for a Christian employer (supervisor, manager, etcetera.). That is because of the unfortunate experiences that they have had in the past.

Such things never should be.

There is more of an onus placed upon the Christian to act justly, than upon their worldly counterparts. We have a responsibility to our workers to treat them in a fair, equitable manner. We should go that extra mile in our treatment of them. We must make sure that the lure of making an extra dollar does not cloud our judgment. If we are only in it to make money, God will not bless us. That is even though we may get rich, sometimes wealthy, in our endeavors. We must be just to all. We should never have the reputation of being hard or unjust. Even a hint of illegality on behalf of the boss, or his company is a disgrace. Our workers should know that we have a care for both their physical well-being as well as their spiritual condition.

The point needs making that this truth applies whether our employees are saved or unsaved. There is a danger we need to be careful to avoid. That is treating our Christian employees different than the unsaved. If we do, we can be charged with nepotism. We are then giving preference to someone not because of what they know or can do. It is because of whom they know and their relationship with us. On the other side, we need to beware that we do not expect more of them and place a higher degree of responsibility on them because they are Christians. We need to make sure we are fair in all of our decisions and how we treat our employees. It must not be just in how we are seen, but how we act.

Separation from the World

There were recent comments made on the subject of showing preference or being partial to any individual. It is to be avoided at all costs. The moment anyone in authority appears to show preference to another their ability to judge impartially is gone. Actions, in this manner, are wrong. We need to make sure that there is not even an appearance of partiality. Even a hint of it will cause the person to lose credibility. It will damage their testimonies. Maybe beyond repair.

If they are saved, our desire should be to see them grow in spiritual things and that their testimonies before both the saved and unsaved should be irreproachable. If our employees are unsaved, we should seek to see them saved and our lives should be such that they will bring glory to the God we profess. Upon their salvation, we should endeavor to see them go on in the things of God. Our testimonies, both inside and outside of the local gathering, should be such that we are without blame amid this wicked, vile generation.

So we are given in this the injunction against a political yoke. As we read, let us obey all its details. Let us be so careful that we do not get caught up into the web of this world's politics and political intrigues. We are to keep separate from all that has to do with it. Even the world has a saying that tells us,

> "Power corrupts, and absolute power corrupts absolutely."

Listen to the unsaved as they speak of politicians. They refer to even the best of them with contempt.

These are several sayings about politicians in this world.

> "Every two years the American politics industry fills the airwaves with the most virulent, scurrilous, wall-to-wall character assassination of nearly every political practitioner in the country – and then declares itself puzzled that America has lost trust in its politicians." – Charles Krauthammer

Joseph John Bowman

Another commentator said,

> "Instead of giving a politician the keys to the city, it might be better to change the lock." – Doug Larson

One of the men with the highest intellects of the previous century said,

> "All of us who are concerned for peace and triumph of reason and justice must be keenly aware of how small an influence reason and good will exert upon events in the political field.' – Albert Einstein

One of the greatest politicians of the past said the following. It sums up all that we know about both politics as well as politicians.

> "Whenever a man casts a longing eye on offices, a rottenness begins in his conduct." – Thomas Jefferson

Let us not be numbered amongst them.

CONCLUSION

In concluding this critical paper, I want to state empirically that no Christian has any right being in politics. That is either by voting or participating as a politician. This exclusion in no way prohibits a Christian from working as an employee for a government agency. However, that is only to be a job and not the manner of life for the believer. There is a federal provision that has recently been mentioned. By its action, it stops any government employee from entering into the political spectrum while in their job. It is called the Hatch Act of 1939. It is US law; It might not be enforced in other countries. However, any believer who is working in these fields should abide by its prohibitions. We are to resist any temptation to get involved in the affairs of the political world.

The Hatch Act states,

> "United States federal law whose main provision prohibits employees in the executive branch of the federal government, except the president, vice-president, and certain designated high-level officials, from engaging in some forms of political activity."

There is a practical reason why employees of the federal government are forbidden to take a side. They are to serve every political party elected. It is not for them to assign loyalties to any particular party or person. They are to be politically impartial.

If there is care to maintain an impartial attitude on behalf of government employees, how much more for the King of Heaven. We are not to be giving our loyalties to any earthly person or party. Our

Joseph John Bowman

loyalty is to Heaven. Those around us should never have any doubt who our King is, and whom we follow. We are not to be tied to the failures and successes of anyone on earth. Our union is with He who made Heaven and earth.

We also need to be very careful where we work and what we do that all that we do will be for the glory of God.

In this paper, I gave examples from the past as to how God looks at the politics of this world. Right, from the Tower of Babel, and before, God hated political entities, because they rose up in rebellion against Him, and His government over man.

I gave the example of how the Nazarite was to separate himself unto the Lord. He was to engage in no worldly joys and to suffer shame in this world. He was to keep himself pure unto His God.

The separation of Abraham shows us that he was to separate himself politically, socially, and religiously from the people of the land. Nothing of the land was to cling to his person or those with whom he would fellowship.

Lastly, we came to the separation found in Second Corinthians 6 Verses 14 to the end. There were five different aspects of separation that the believer was enjoined to keep. They were commercial separation, social separation, religious separation, marital separation, and political separation. While covering them all, I dealt most extensively with the political aspect. It is neglected today. Worse than that, political stands are embraced and celebrated by the Church.

Under political separation, Christ is our Leader, and Belial is the leader of this world. We looked at our responsibility to the government and closed with our responsibility to the union in the workplace. The last is an area that has been very much neglected in the last few years and needs to be dealt with as it is an area that has affected our testimonies to our unsaved workmates.

Separation from the World

I trust as we look at this paper, we will look at it in light of what the Word of God has to say and not to accept it or reject it because I said it.

> "Study to shew thyself approved unto God, a workman that needeth not to be ashamed, rightly dividing the Word of Truth" (2 Tim. 2:15).

I want to thank you for your patience and consideration while going over these few thoughts. I want to leave with Paul's exhortation to Timothy. As we read it, take everything written in light of the Word of God. That is the only way anything said can have any authority. It is the Word of God that is our final stand. If it is not there, all we have is the opinions of men. In the end, my opinions are no better than what anybody else thinks.

Here is an acid test we all should use in the Scriptures,

> "Consider what I say: and the Lord give thee understanding in all things" (2 Tim. 2:7).

That is the only way that we will learn anything that is from God. We need the Lord through the power of the Holy Spirit to teach us the things of God. Only then will we understand the deep things of God. In the end, this should be the desire of the hearts of each one of us.

FINIS

He Whom we love and worship is overall. He is God Almighty. We can rest sure in the fact that all things are under His control. We need not fret or worry about the affairs of this earth. No matter how bad things get, we know that God is still in control. At the end of this book, I want to give a few words from others about their estimation of the Son of God. At the same time, I want to leave with a few verses of Scripture dealing with the power of God and His authority over this world. Let us keep this in mind as we seek to live down here.

Our responsibility is not to seek to change this world but to accept what we see as in His will. We must be witnesses for Him amid a wicked world. By doing so, we desire to seek souls saved and brought into His heavenly kingdom. We are not to change things in the world that has been cursed by God. We are to bring out from it souls for Him.

Theodulf of Orleans wrote the first hymn quoted. Charlemagne made him the Bishop of Orleans. After Charlemagne's death, he was imprisoned in Anger, France for conspiring against King Louis the Pious. He wrote the words to this hymn while in a dungeon around the year 820 A.D. He was released shortly after its composition. However, he died shortly after his release. It has been used a processional hymn on Palm Sunday.

Joseph John Bowman

All Glory, Laud, and Honor

All glory, laud, and honor
To You, Redeemer, King
To Whom the lips of children
Made sweet hosannas ring.
You are the King of Israel
And David's Royal Son,
Now in the Lord's name coming,
The King and blessed One

The company of angels
Is praising You on high;
And we with all creation
In chorus make reply.
The people of the Hebrews
With palms before You went;
Our praise and prayer and anthems
Before You we present.

To You before Your passion
They sang their hymns of praise;
To You, now high exalted,
Our melody we raise.
As You received their praises,
Accept the prayers we bring,
For You delight in goodness,
O Good and Gracious King!

Theodulph, Bishop of Orleans

Translator

J. M. Neale

The Psalmist spoke as he described the God whom he served. He saw
Him as the One who was overall.

Separation from the World

"The Lord is in His holy temple, the Lord's throne is in Heaven: His eyes behold, His eyelids try, the children of men" (Ps. 11:4).

Again,

"All the ends of the world shall remember and turn unto the Lord: and all kindreds of the nations shall worship before Thee. For the kingdom is the Lord's: and He is the governor among the nations" (Ps. 22:27-28).

We have this Psalm where our God is extolled over the earth.

"The earth is the Lord's, and the fulness thereof: the world, and they that dwell therein" (Ps.24:1).

He follows by telling us majestic things about God. He is shown as the King triumphant. No other entity, either in Heaven or earth or under the earth is His equal. He will reign over all.

He finishes this Psalm,

"Lift up your heads, O ye gates: and be ye lift up, ye everlasting doors: and the King of glory shall come in. Who is this King of glory? The Lord strong and mighty, the Lord mighty in battle. Lift up your heads. O ye gates: even lift them up, ye everlasting doors: and the King of glory shall come in. Who is this King of glory? The Lord of hosts, He is the King of glory. Selah" (Ps. 24:7-10).

Habakkuk compares Him to the idols of this world. He started by saying,

"Woe unto him that saith to the wood, Awake: to the dumb stone, Arise, it shall teach! Behold, it is laid over with gold and silver, and there is no breath at all in the midst of it. But the Lord is in His holy temple: let all the earth keep silence before Him" (Hab. 2:19-20).

Joseph John Bowman

I want to give another hymn with uncertain date of authorship. The initials only indicate the writer. The writer has given no precise indication of their authorship or when he wrote the hymn. We do know that Clement W. Poole wrote the music for the hymn. He died in 1828,

His words give no doubt about the power and authority of Him whom they are telling us.

The Man on the Throne

We gather here remembering,
Lord, You are all in all.
Our hearts cry out in love toward You,
In all creation too.
You are the meaning of our life,
Of all we are and do.

You captivated us and now
We follow in Your train,
We are Your people, You're our God
In us do rule and reign,
You are the Man upon the Throne
Set there by God alone,
God planned and willed that You be Head
The Lord of all made known.

Those God foreknew, He set apart
To be confirmed to You,
That You would be His Firstborn Son
And we Your brothers true,
You conquered death and rose with might
Ascending to the height.
You carry out God's will on earth,
Enthroned in glory bright.

Separation from the World

Lord, as the God-exalted man,
The Ruler of all kings,
Your government fulfills God's plan,
And utmost Headship brings
You, as God's Heir, uphold all things,
Our heart in worship sings.
You make God's substance known by all
As from Your Throne life springs.

Our Pioneer and Forerunner,
You clearly cut the way
Unto God's Throne and reign by life,
To this "Amen," we say,
You take the lead, and we follow You.
No other way will do,
For God intends to glorify
And seat us there with You.

Under the ruling of Your life,
We too will reign as kings,
Saved by Your grace abundantly,
Upheld on eagles wings.
God's gift of righteousness received
By us who have believed,
We'll testify eternally
Your rule is all we need.

L.S.

I want to close this section with one more hymn which describes Who it is we serve. It will end with telling us not only how man sees Him but how God sees Him.

Joseph John Bowman

O Worship the King, All Glorious Above

O worship the King all glorious above,
O gratefully sing His power and His love:
Our shield and defender, The Ancient of Days,
Pavilioned in splendor and girded with praise.

O tell of His might, O sing of His grace,
Whose robe is the light, whose canopy space,
His chariots of wrath the deep thunderclouds form,
And dark is the path on the wings of the storm.

The earth, with its store of wonders untold,
Almighty, Thy power hath founded of old,
Hath stablished it fast by a changeless decree,
And round it hath cast, like a mantle the sea.

Thy bountiful care what tongue can recite?
It breathes in the air, it shines in the light,
It streams from the hills, it descends to the plain,
And sweetly distills in the dew and the rain.

Frail children of dust, and feeble as frail,
In Thee do we trust, nor find Thee to fail,
Thy mercies how tender, how firm to the end,
Our Maker, Defender, Redeemer, and Friend.

Sir Robert Grant

Sir Robert Grant became a lawyer in 1807. In 1834 he was given the position of Judge Advocate General of England. Later, he was appointed Governor of Bombay, India and after that knighted. As a result of his service for England, he wrote this hymn. He recognized that there was One over all earthly authorities to whom he was accountable. We have those on earth to whom we owe our obedience and allegiance. However, there is One whose power and authority are

Separation from the World

far overall. He is the One whom we owe all homage and devotion. I will close this section with the following verses.

> "Wherefore God also hath highly exalted Him and given Him a name which is above every name: that at the name of Jesus every knee should bow, of things in Heaven, and things in earth, and things under the earth: and that every tongue should confess that Jesus Christ is Lord, to the glory of God the Father" (Phil. 2:9-11).

The last viewpoint I want to give is of Him coming out of Heaven to rule this earth. There is none like Him, and there has been no one comparable to Him. He is the incomparable One.

> "And I saw heaven opened, and behold a white horse: and He that sat upon him was called Faithful and True, and in righteousness, He doth judge and makes war. His eyes were as a flame of fire, and His head wore many crowns: and he had a name written, that no man knew, but He Himself. Moreover, He was clothed with a vesture dipped in blood: and His name is called The Word of God. And the armies which were in Heaven followed Him upon white horses, clothed in fine linen, white and clean. And out of His mouth goeth a sharp sword, that with it He should smite the nations: and He shall rule them with a rod of iron: and He treadeth the winepress of the fierceness and wrath of Almighty God. And He hath on His vesture and on His thigh a name written, KING OF KINGS, AND LORD OF LORDS" (Rev. 19:11-16).

How can we ever place our hope and confidence in any other ruler? If He is our hope and salvation, how can we follow anyone else? What reason do we have to think that any earthly ruler, king, or president can effect changes or policies that God will not allow or sanction? How will any earthly ruler be able to put into effect any policies that God does not desire? If these statements are true, how dare we align ourselves alongside any other power than that which is from God?

CULMINATION

I want to thank all who have stayed with this critical subject. I recognize that it is exceptionally controversial on both sides. The majority of believers not only vote; they also take exception to believers who refrain from doing so. Most of these believers are convinced that it is inconceivable a just God would allow the wickedness and lawless activities on this earth to go unchecked. They feel that we have a responsibility to act as a restraining influence on those in power. One Scripture they go to often deals with the words of the Lord Jesus.

He said concerning His followers,

> "Ye are the salt of the earth" (Matt. 5:13).

Now among other things, salt stops food from corrupting. They teach this is our work in the world. We are to be a force to stop the corruption that is going on around us. That is true, and it is part of our duties. However, we need to realize the context of His words. The Lord was telling those around that not only are they to be the salt of the earth, but they are the light of the world (Matt. 5:14). As the salt, we are representatives of the righteous requirements of God. As the light, we are to be testimonies of Him who called us out of the darkness of this world. In both ways, we are to fulfill our activities without becoming part of the systems that God hates. We are not to be partners with them in their wicked deeds. Even association with them is a tacit acknowledgment that they have our approval. We need to carefully guard the specialness and moral characters of our testimony before Him. Never let it be suggested that for the sake of expediency, we compromised a truth of Scripture.

Joseph John Bowman

We must keep in mind the final reason we are here. It is not only to witness to the unsaved, but it is to live lives acceptable in the sight of Almighty God. We are to live in light of the day when we will be absent from the body and present with the Lord (2 Cor. 5:8). Our aim should be on that Day we will be found acceptable in His sight. The hymn writer was viewing all of the trials and disappointments of life in the following hymn. As he did so, he put everything into perspective by looking at what lay before. His thoughts were as David's when he saw the prosperity of the wicked. David was puzzled and wondered why the wicked seemed to win while the righteous suffered persecution.

"Until I went into the sanctuary of God: then understood I their end" (Ps.73:17).

The next hymn takes us into the Sanctuary of God. There we find all we need and the reasons for everything that has occurred on earth. We will lack for nothing and wonder no more. The prospect that lies before each believer should be enough to give us the impetus to move forward in time.

My Rest is in Heaven

My rest is in Heaven, my rest is not here,
Then why should I murmur when trials are near?
Be hushed my sad spirit, the worst that can come
But shortens the journey and hastens me Home.

It is not for me to be seeking my bliss,
And building my hopes in a region like this;
I look for a City which hands have not piled;
I pant for a Country by sin undefiled.

The winds of affliction around me may blow,
And dash my lone barque as I'm sailing below;
I smile at the storm as I lean on His breast,
And soon I shall land in the Haven of Rest.

Separation from the World

Let trial and danger my progress oppose,
They only make Heaven more sweet at the close;
Come joy or come sorrow, whate'er may befall,
A Home with my God will make up for it all.

With Christ in my heart, and His Word in my hand,
I travel in haste through an enemy's land;
The road may be rough, but it cannot be long,
So I journey on singing the Conqueror's song.

Henry Francis Lyte

BIBLIOGRAPHY

1. A.B. – The Mystery of Phanaticism – 1698
2. Aesop – Quotation – 620 – 564 B.C.
3. All Glory, Laud, and Honor – Theodulf, Bishop of Orleans – 820 A.D. Translated by J. M. Neale 1854 A. D.
4. All to Jesus I Surrender – William Williams Pentycelyn – 1717-1791
5. Anonymous – Public Domain – None but Christ
6. Bacon, Francis – Viscount St Alban – The Essays: Of Atheism - 1601
7. Banneker, Benjamin – Quotation – 1731-1806
8. Bennett, Lucy, Anne – 1850-1927 – Holy, Happy Separation
9. Bombeck, Erma – Book Title – 1978
10. Bowring, John – In the Cross of Christ I Glory – 1825
11. Chung, Anne – Quotation
12. Churchill, Winston – Quotation – 1948
13. Darby, John, Nelson – 1800- 1862 – This World is a Wilderness Wide
14. Einstein, Albert – Quotation
15. Fausset, A. R. Rev. – Jamieson, Fausett, and Brown – 1871
16. Funston. Elizabeth - Quotation
17. Gesenius, Wilheim – 1786-1842 – Gesenius' Hebrew and Chaldee Lexicon – Translated by – Samuel P. Tregelles – 1813-1875
18. Billy, Rev. – 1918-2018 – Quotations
19. Grant, Robert – Oh Worship the King – 1833
20. Grigg, Joseph – 1722-1768 – Jesus! And Shall it Ever Be – Altered by Benjamin Francis – 1734-1799
21. Hatch Act of 1939 – An Act to Prevent Pernicious Political Activities – Quotation
22. Havergal, Frances, Ridley – Take My Life and let it Be – 1874
23. Heber, Reginald – Holy, Holy, Holy! Lord God Almighty – 1826

Joseph John Bowman

24. Hoffman, Elisha J. – 1839-1929 – I've Turned My Back upon the World
25. Hislop, Alexander, Rev. – The Two Babylons – 1858
26. Jefferson, Thomas – Quotation
27. Krauthammer, Charles – Quotation
28. Larson, Doug – Quotation
29. Lyte, Henry, Francis – 1793-1847 – My Rest is in Heaven
30. Moore, Thomas – 1779-1852 – Sound the High Praises of Jesus the King
31. Niebuhr, Reinhold – 1892-1971 - The Serenity Prayer – Alcoholics Anonymous Prayer -
32. Newberry, Thomas – The Englishman's Bible – The Newberry Bible – Printed in Great Britain at the University Press, Oxford
33. Oatman, Johnson, Jr. – Count Your Blessings – 1897
34. Open Doors USA – Article – Christian Persecution
35. Pope, Alexander – "An Essay on Criticism" – 1688-1744
36. Powell, Colin – 4 Star General (ret.) – 1937 – Quotations
37. Prakash, Ajai – Pastor, Author – Sermon – January 5, 2011
38. RSV Version – Quotation – Rom. 10:9
39. S. L. – The Man on the Throne
40. Santayana, George – Quotation – 1905
41. Strong, James L.L.D. Std. – Strong's Exhaustive Concordance of the Bible – Abingdon Press, 43rd Printing, 1984
42. Suffield, Kittie – Hymn – Chorus – God is Still on the Throne – 1929
43. Spurgeon. Charles – Quotation
44. Tennyson, Alfred, Lord – The Charge of the Light Brigade – 1854
45. The Phrase Finder – Online – Quotation – Proverb
46. Toronto Sun – Article – Quote by Professor Antonella Artuso – University of Toronto – 2016
47. Quotation – Proverb – The Phrase Finder – Online
48. Unknown – Quotation
49. Unknown Author - Hymn
50. Wooding, Dan – Article on Chinese Persecution

BIOGRAPHY

I want to give a brief biography of who I am, and with what I am currently involved. I was born Joseph John Bowman on June 7, 1955, in Trail, British Columbia, Canada of Christian parents, John and Anne Bowman. That is to say; there was a time in both of their lives when they accepted the Lord Jesus Christ as their own personal Saviour. That did not prepare me for Heaven. There had to come a time when I accepted the work finished on the cross as my own. When He paid the penalty for sin, He died for me. That time came on a Sunday night in November 1962 in Fairview, Alberta, Canada. My mother led me to the Lord, showing me that I was a sinner and that Christ died for me. The verse God used to show me His salvation was;

> "I am the door: by Me if any man enter in he shall
> be saved, and shall go in and out and find pasture"
> (John 10:9).

That night I saw Jesus Christ as the Door to Heaven, and I entered in through the Door. If you have not seen Him as the only way to Heaven and entered in do so today for His name's sake. He is the One who said,

> "I am the way, the truth, and the life: no man cometh
> unto the Father but by Me" (John 14:6).

He is the only way! I entered into that way on that night at the age of seven and had been traveling to Heaven ever since. What joy has been mine in the years that have passed!

Joseph John Bowman

At the age of thirteen, on September 16, 1968, I was baptized by immersion in the Columbia River in fellowship with the Christians that met together in the Fifth and Elm Gospel Hall in Castlegar, British Columbia, Canada. The following June I was received into the fellowship of the Saints there.

When I was fifteen, my father passed into the presence of the Lord he had loved and served for many years. There were some hard years after that. Later, I moved to Edmonton, Alberta, and briefly attended the Mount Carmel Bible School. While there, I learned different truths. I soon learned that spiritual truths are taught in God's gathering place by God-ordained men in God's time and God's way. His truths do not come as a crash course over one year or four-year programs. It takes a lifetime to learn the things of God.

From there I went to the Connor's Hill Gospel Hall in Edmonton, Alberta, Canada, and was received into fellowship in September 1977. On June 30, 1978, I married Joanie Stewart, who is now my wife of over forty years. Joanie was in fellowship in the West End Gospel Hall in Winnipeg, Manitoba, Canada. (Now the Parksview Gospel Hall.) Her parents Norman, and Janet Stewart were members there the whole of their Christian lives. They passed into the presence of the Lord a few years ago. The Lord blessed us with two sons and seven grandchildren. (As well we have three grandchildren waiting for us in Heaven.) How we pray for our grandchildren's salvation while young in life.

I have been privileged to serve as both an evangelist as well as a teacher for many years.

I began writing a few years ago at the encouragement of a sister in the Lord and have sought to serve in this area since then. I trust that God will bless this work for Him as I seek to present different aspects of Church truth to the people of God.